ZERO TO SUPERHERO

JASON S. COMELY

ISBN 978-1-4357-0055-0

DISCLAIMER

Zero to Superhero is not intended to replace medical advice offered by physicians.

Reference the information contained herein with other reliable sources, and consult your professional health care provider before taking any course of action.

Oh, and have fun with it.

PREFACE

Zero to Superhero is not really about transforming into a vigilante crime fighter and stalking the streets under the cover of night. Becoming a superhero is a metaphor for realizing your full potential and having a positive influence in your sphere of influence. Being strong and healthy requires balance in one's life and the constant development of physical, mental and spiritual muscles. I say that being physically overweight does not debar a person from being a *real* superhero, nor does a low GPA exclude one from having wisdom and the ability to dispense good advice.

The underscoring theme of the book is this: whether you're blasting your biceps in the gym, preparing a meal, or listening to a child's story, give your undivided attention to the task at hand. Wring every last drop out of your time and abilities. Most of all, go outside of you and ease the suffering of others. That's being a real superhero.

YOUTUBE MEETS ZERO TO SUPERHERO

Zero to Superhero is like no other fitness book, not only because of it's high-energy writing style and unconventional wisdom, but because it leverages the power of YouTube™ and the unconventional wisdom of people like you. You'll notice that some sections reference specific YouTube™ videos I thought added valuable information or even a little "je ne sais quoi" for texture. It's an experiment that I hope works.

Maybe you can do better, and if that's the case, point me to your video and I may publish it in the book!

THANK YOU

As I look back on the four plus years of researching, experimenting, testing and writing this book, I recognize there were important people along the way who helped bring me to the finish line. Janet Cain comes quickly to mind as the fireball motivator from Chicago who pushed hard for results. She's a heck of a girl and I've dedicated the book to her. Thank you Janet. Cristina (codename: Catwoman) is another person of notable awesomeness who provided ideas and suggestions. My brothers Corey and Jordan stepped up with artwork, as well as my dad - the creator of Canada's superhero Captain Canuck. Thanks and love are in order.

Props also to my college buddy Preston Roberts who was there on the clutch for the initial cover scans, and Kevin Williams (a.k.a. WordSmythe) for his sage advice and support.

Above all I want to express my love to my three beautiful daughters: Desire, Brielle and Sierra.

Finally, this book would not be possible without the help of God. He lives, and Jesus Christ is the living Son of God and the Savior of the world. (Note: This is not a Christian fitness book or anything like that, it just had to be said. Thank you for allowing me).

ABOUT THE AUTHOR

Jason S Comely is a fitness enthusiast who was educated in fitness theory and personal training at Mohawk College in Ontario, Canada. He enjoys running, mountain biking and resistance training (which is the term to use when you're not sure whether to put weightlifting or bodybuilding) as well as doing fatherly things with his three children. Zero to Superhero is his first book.

Visit **ZerotoSuperhero.com** for more information.

REFERENCES AND BONUS MATERIAL

Since Zero to Superhero paperback is currently a print-by-demand publication, cost per unit is considerable. To keep the value of the book high and priced inexpensively for the consumer, I've decided not to include a reference section in the book, but rather have it be available on request. This also includes Dangerous Curves Ahead, the chapter written exclusively for women. It is available to you, the purchaser of this book, free of charge. Simply email me at admin@zerotosuperhero.com and I'll promptly reply to you with the pdf file attached

Thank you for purchasing the book, and I wish you many great and wonderful changes in your life.

CONTENTS

PREFACE

APPETITE FOR REDUCTION

THE CRISIS

A widespread outbreak is sweeping the planet. It's an unfortunate and preventable disposition that affects the rich and the poor, hero and villain, the young and the restless. It's obesity, and along with its paradoxical accomplice under-nutrition, this deadly duo can be a killer.

THE PLAN

The best defense against this global epidemic is empowering yourself with knowledge, and the best place to start are you. Know what your BMR, BMI and maintenance calories are. Then, and only then, are you ready to learn insider tactics of attacking fat and staying lean.

BASIC METABOLIC RATE (BMR)

Basic Metabolic Rate represents the minimum caloric intake you need for boring stuff like breathing, heart beat, blood flow and body temperature regulation. Basic Metabolic Rate is *not* the same as "maintenance calories" (see below) because no activities above and beyond basic physiological functioning in a resting state are included, while maintenance calories is the total caloric needs for all normal everyday activities. It's also not to be confused with the Body Mass Indicator (BMI – also below). You can figure out your BMR by using this formula:

BODYWEIGHT (LBS) X (11 FOR MALE, 10 FOR FEMALE) / 24.

This means multiply your weight (in lbs) by either 11 or 10 and divide the number by 24 (24 being the number of hours in a day natch). P.S. This number will prove to be indispensable, as you'll need to know your BMR to calculate the MET values for various world saving activities.

MAINTENANCE CALORIES

As stated above, your maintenance calories is how many calories are required for you to operate effectively in an average day, without gaining or losing weight. It encompasses the energy requirements of all typical physiological processes as well as the caloric demands of work, rest and play. To figure this magical number out requires documenting every morsel that touches your lips for three days. Have a calorie counter book and a notepad handy, and write down how much you ate of what, and how many calories it was. At the end of each day, tally up the calories and at the end of the three days add it all up and divide the gargantuan number by three:

CAL TOTAL FROM DAY ONE + DAY TWO + DAY THREE / THREE = MAINTENANCE CALORIES

Actually, this reminds me of a diet trick: Documenting on paper every bite of food has a way of discouraging unnecessary snacking that can pile up the calories. Try this and see if it doesn't make eating an inconvenience you would rather avoid. By documenting everything you eat, you also recognize the times you eat for reasons other than being hungry (e.g. bored, lonely, stressed out). People will sometimes use food as a form of entertainment, or even as a passive response to advertisements from shadowy multi-national conglomerates. Could this be the shocking revelation as to why North Americans eat an average of 115 extra calories every Friday, Saturday and Sunday as a study has shown?! By the end of the weekend, we've

inhaled 345 "bonus" calories (and probably not the healthy kind either). Diabolical!

You Tube

Title: **How to Calculate Calories Burned**

Tags: calories exercise fitness basal metabolic rate weight loss training energy expenditure

From: NewsTeamBoulder

THREE SIMPLE HEALTH INDICATORS

The Body Mass Index (BMI) has been accepted as the de facto indicator of general health according to height and weight, and has been used for over 100 years by hospitals, employers, fitness clubs, insurance companies and drug manufacturers. Unfortunately, it sucks with extreme vorticity because the measurement doesn't account for body composition - specifically whether any weight over the "norm" is muscle or fat. Muscle is denser than fat, so according to the BMI, many muscular people are incorrectly classified as overweight (*if you're not sure whether it relates to you, here's a test. Look in the mirror. If you have no neck, the BMI isn't for you*).

According to Tim Cole, a professor of medical statistics, a far more accurate indicator of physical well-being is a Waist Circumference Measurement (WCM), since health problems occur when the surplus weight is fat and it is accumulated in the hips and abdominal area. Men with a waistband of more than 37 inches (94 cm) and women thicker than 32 cm (80 cm) are at an increased risk of cardiovascular and metabolic disease.

Wait. There's yet another test devised by German and Austrian researchers which also works on the waistband principle and it's called the <u>Waist-to-Tallness Ratio</u> (WTR). With this test, men shoot for a WTR of 0.55 or less and women 0.53 or below. To determine what your waist should be for your height, take your height in inches and multiply it by 0.55 for men and 0.53 for women.

Anyway, if you're still interested in the BMI as a standard point of reference, here's how to read it. The American Institute for Cancer Research claims anywhere from 18.5 to 25 to be ideal for a civilian, while anything 25 to 29.9 is considered overweight. Individuals are considered obese anywhere above a score of 30.

Here is a way of determining your BMI "score":

You need to know your height in meters. You can do this by dividing your height (in inches) by 39.36.

If your weight in pounds, divide your weight by 2.2 to determine your weight in kilograms.

Square your height (in meters). To square a number means to multiply the number by itself.

Finally, divide your weight (which you figured into kilograms) by your squared height to get your BMI reading.

> Dirt Simple: Your waist size (in inches) should be one half of your overall height or less.

4

CALORIC RESTRICTION VS MACRO-NUTRIENT MANIPULATION

This is where it gets interesting, if not controversial. I believe, through empirical data and various texts, that you can reduce body fat simply by manipulating macro-nutrient ratios. Make no other changes in your daily routine - not

caloric intake, not activity level, nada - and you will rid adipose tissue (a fancy lad way of saying fat) by altering macro-nutrient ratios ala the Keto-Fu Plan I spun from other similar diet plans. Naysayer's will state creating a caloric deficit is the only effective way one can lose weight, but that's so badly oversimplifying the situation, it's flat-out wrong. Here's why:

- Insulin is the hormone responsible for fat storage, and eating high-glycemic foods cause dramatic insulin spikes which will encourage adipose and prevent you from burning fat, no matter how low your caloric intake. Low-glycemic foods don't trigger a significant insulin response, so you can eat more calories and still lose weight. Heck, you'll be burning body fat all the live long day eating low-glycemic foods.

- Understanding, harnessing and controlling powerful hormones in your own body is fundamental in losing body fat and keep it off easily, without suffering pangs of hunger. We discussed elsewhere in the book about the hormone insulin, which needs to be caged up and only unleashed at optimal times, but there are other hormones that affect metabolism and can easily be manipulated by diet. Testosterone and Insulin like Growth Factor (IGF) are two prime examples. Diets high in protein and good fats promote higher levels of these hormones critical to muscle growth and subsequent fat loss due to a higher metabolism.

- Food combining, as popularized by the Fit for Life ™ plan, is still relevant. It goes a little something like this: you can eat protein and carbs together, but not fat, OR protein and fat together, but not carbs, but it's important not to combine carbs and fat together because the ingested carbohydrates will be converted to sugar for quick energy and the fat stored away into fat cells. Generally, any food not needed for immediate energy is converted to stored body fat (the exception being ketosis, which makes fat storage metabolically impossible because body fat is being utilized as fuel. Access fat is passed through the urine instead).

- Frequent eating has a way of keeping the metabolism ticking and cortisol levels down (cortisol is a stress hormone produced by the adrenal glands, that can destroy hard-earned muscle and aid in body fat acquisition). When you're hungry, bet the farm cortisol levels are up. Six or more small meals spread out over a day gives your body a continual supply of nutrients and can prevent binge eating resulting from caloric deprivation.

- The Germans have a phrase that goes "*eat breakfast like a king, lunch like a common-folk and dinner like a beggar*", which, translated in English, means caloric intake should taper off as it gets closer to your beauty sleep, and carbohydrate intake low to nil with your last meal.

I hope I've made my point, but in a gesture of peace I extend this olive branch to those in the "caloric-restriction-or-the-highway" camp: *any* diet including the Keto-Fu Plan is definitely more effective when a mild caloric deficit is created. It's not mandatory for success, but it's highly recommended and a smaller appetite is usually a natural bi-product of dieting anyway.

CALORIC RESTRICTION WITH OPTIMAL NUTRITION (CRON)

It's been calculated, based on animal studies, that for every calorie denied, 30 seconds of extra life is added. For

example, forsaking an original Burger King Whopper with all the fixing's will give you almost an extra six hours to live. Still not impressed? Consider then the prediction that caloric restriction (CR) could, in an ancillary way, extend the life of humans to 1000 years! Aubrey de grey, an age theorist and gene database manager at Cambridge University, predicts that while caloric restriction adds only a modest amount of years, forth-coming first generation rejuvenation therapies will compliment and compound our life spans further. This in turn will buy more time in which there will hopefully be better therapies and extend lives longer still, perhaps even a millennium.

There's more. Along with extension of years, calorie-restriction subjects dramatically reduce their risk of heart disease and of having a stroke or diabetes. These disciples of denial and their 1000 – 2000 calorie diets have lower bodyfat and oft higher energy levels than their 2000 – 3550+ calorie consuming cohorts. But how are these benefits accrued from eating less energy? Plausible hypotheses abound, from metabolic down-regulation, less oxidative damage (due to less sugars, additives, sugars and pesticides ingested), developmental delay, to a defensive anti-aging response called hormesis which is caused by the low-intensity biological stress that is imposed

7

by caloric restriction. Whatever the reason (perhaps all these theories could be right), CR has been proven effective in numerous animal studies, and the quest to attaining similar physiological benefits in humans is currently underway.

So you're considering caloric restriction? Granted, under the right conditions caloric restriction can be all that and a side order of organic carrot sticks, but it can easily lead to malnutrition and result in serious lifelong ailments when not done properly. It's important to know some serious stuff before embarking on a CR program:

1) Caloric restriction is NOT suitable for children. Children need lots of calories to sponsor their growing bodies and the many activities they engage in. Caloric restriction can be appropriate for adults, but check with your doctor first. Should your doctor give the green light, it's recommended you practice caloric restriction under the osmosis of a registered dietician to determine appropriate macronutrient ratios for your lifestyle and body and blood type.

2) Nutrient-dense foods and vitamin supplementation are vital when calories are scarce, which is why Caloric Restriction is often referred to as CRAN or CRON (caloric restriction with adequate/optimal nutrition). Load up on raw, unprocessed foods rich in antioxidants with a short shipping time from grower to grocery. Why? Because some oranges from the local supermarket have virtually no vitamin C in them at all, due to the mind-reeling length of time transporting and storing them! Opt for lean sources of protein and back away from grain products which are more filler and no real nutritional value.

3) Caloric restriction needs to be implemented gradually, with special emphasis on fulfilling vitamin, mineral and enzymatic requisites. In animal studies, sudden switches to caloric restriction not only failed to extend the life of the test subject, but sometimes even shortened it! The key is to gently reduce calories over an 8-12 week period, deficit no more than 5% total caloric intake per week. Along with this is the fact that since many chemicals and toxins are fat soluble and bind to bodyfat, over-aggressive fat loss would release too much toxins into the circulatory system and make you ill and weak.

4) Caloric restrictive programs CRON/CRAN are a long term commitment, a lifestyle change. They are not short term diets to quickly drop some weight and

5) resume normal eating habits again. Rest assured, to do so would be to sabotage yourself and make you fatter than before! Why is this? It has to do with survival mechanisms of the body. When the body feels threatened it's not getting enough calories, it creates fat-storing A2 adrenoreceptors which predominate in the usual problem areas (midsection for men, butt and thighs for women), so when the body does finally receive more calories, it can sequester more away as fat – just in case you try that stupid trick again. You will have then accumulated more bodyfat than if you'd not tried it at all!

6) While studies on mice offered proof that caloric restriction prolongues lifespan, it also showed that the mice undergoing the diet fared worse on tests relating to memory and spatial learning. Be warned, caloric restriction may hinder your ability to perform certain mentally demanding tasks and make you susceptible to evil mind rays.

But regardless of whether and however you throttle caloric intake, numerous studies show leanness and avoiding the accumulation of access bodyfat can extend your lifespan. Leanness typically means longer life!

Title: **Exploring life extension part 3 caloric restriction**

Tags: transhumanism life extension immortality future society

From: norton420

FASTING? NOT SO FAST!

THE GOOD:

- The ever-expanding multi-national pharmaceutical companies would have us believe there's a pill for everything that ails us, which biotechnology will save us all. But the jarring truth is we will never match wits with our Maker, who made our bodies more self sustainable than this consumer-mad culture would ever want you to know. Fasting is nature's way of cleansing and resting the body. No pill or machine can heal the body; only the body can heal itself. To quote Voltaire: "The art of medicine consists of amusing the patient, while nature cures the disease."

  So what do you do if you're feeling ill? Loren Lockman, founder and director of the Tanglewood Wellness Center says to do what over 25 million animal species do when under the weather, they "lie down and refuse food" until substantially recovered.

"Often, when people are sick, they lose their appetite," Loren writes in the Tanglewood guidebook. "In our culture, we often encourage them to eat to 'keep up their strength'. Unwittingly, we are further teaching them to *not* follow their instincts and intuition."

"Unlike medicine – both conventional and alternative – fasting is about actually healing the body, rather than simply treating symptoms... Healing is an inherent power of every living organism. Fasting simply provides the body - any body – with the optimal conditions and opportunity to cleanse itself of accumulated toxins, and heal any prior damage."

Loren goes on to state the digestive tract spends approximately 50% of the bodies daily energy. Relieving the body of that constant stress from time to time by abstaining from food is obviously of physiological benefit.

- While instant self-gratification and over-consumerism is bringing the world to its knees, fasting allows us to elevate the spirit and develop mastery over our appetites. The body yields to the will, and temporal needs are de-prioritized. Fasting also helps us have a better appreciation for food, not only because eating seems more flavorful and purposeful when we break the fast, but because there are many in the world that are denied food.

- Fasting for a 24 hour period (no food, no water) stimulates the secretion of growth hormone, the key hormone that keeps you looking young and healthy. I've heard some male models will fast once a month to thwart Old Man Time

AND THE BAD:

- It's been said the best way to fatten up livestock is to starve them and re-feed them, and such is the confidence-shattering result of fasting when used as a vehicle for weight loss. Prolonged fasting sends the body into producing what are known as A2 adrenoreceptors. Think of these A2 receptors as vacant motel rooms in a seedy part of town, and there's a big neon sign that says "Discounts for triglycerides, weekly and monthly rates available". You get stubborn body fat that checks in and won't leave until the welfare runs out. Worse yet, your body consumes its own muscle mass during an extended fast and essentially destroys your metabolism. From then on, it'll take less food to make you fat. Talk about a backfire!

CRUSH YOUR APPETITE EIGHT WAYS TO SUNDAY

What once seemed good now as turned unspeakably evil, growling deep within the black pit of your stomach. It's your appetite and it's large and in charge, but with these handy tactics and your uncanny discipline, you can stop it before it devours the whole galaxy!

1) Drink water. It's well documented that people who drink lot's of water during and between meals feel more content. Sometimes it's a hard sell on the stomach, which wants something more substantial. If this is this case then...

2) Drink a fiber laxative. Fiber not only helps you feel full, it will help you lose weight and keep your bowels honest. According to the Harvard School of Public Health, adults should consume 20-35 grams of dietary fiber per day, yet the average American consumes only 14-15

grams. That's less than half of the recommended daily intake, so you may already be in the hole. Try one or two rounded teaspoons of non-flavoured Metamucil with water or juice.

3) You may find drinking glutamine dissolved in water when on a carb restrictive diet can help defeat cravings bent on imprisoning you in fatness forever. Glutamine not only gives a feeling of satiation, but helps restore and build muscle tissue, fosters a growth hormone response, and a grocery list of other benefits. And it doesn't add a single calorie. Drink 5-10 grams, several times a day, especially when transitioning into ketosis.

4) I've found listening to jazz or classical music during mealtime tends to allay the appetite, but blasting "Rage against the Machine" through the speakers at 100+ dB to be equally effective. (I've tried it, but I don't recommend it).

5) It could be your taste buds are jonesin' for some excitement. Try adding more spices to your lean meats and vegetables to make your food more flavorful and less forgettable.

6) Vegetables rule when it comes to providing satisfaction, energy and nutrients, so aim for five or more different vegetables a day. The easy way to accomplish to buy pre-packaged, frozen vegetables like California mix or Santa Fe style.

7) Supplementing with omega 3 will help you lose fat, stabilize insulin levels and stops sugar cravings. Take on a teaspoon or two of Omega 3 rich fats like flaxseed or hemp oil and you'll bring the smackdown on the munchies!

8) Try a protein drink with skim milk. Dieting can cause a negative nitrogen balance, which in turn negatively affects muscle development. Less muscle means a slower base metabolism, which means it'll be harder to lose the flab ...and so the tragic cycle continues. Drinking a low carb whey protein drink with skim milk will silence those hunger pangs and won't interrupt your quest to become superhumanly huge and shredded.

SUPPLEMENT SIDEKICK: Native to the tropical regions of India, Gymnema Sylvestre is a vine in the milkweed family and has been used to treat type II diabetes for over 2000 years. It suppresses sweet tooth cravings (its Hindi name is gurmar, meaning "destroyer of sugar") and lowers high blood glucose levels, a condition known as hyperglycemia. Take 150 mg Gymnema extract standardized two times a day.

10 STRATEGIES TO STOKING THE METABOLISM

If you're on a caloric-restrictive diet and feel weak as Superman wearing kryptonite bling, it's likely because your body countered by down regulating in metabolism. However, there are ways to outsmart your body and fire up the metabolism.

1. THE WAY TO WAKE

Want to start your day on the right side of the bed? Wake up at sunrise, when darkness dispels and the natural light of day begins. Chronobiologists, scientists who study the effects of time and circadian rhythms, say waking up at sunrise stimulates a whole host of positive hormonal activity including serotonin and adrenaline and suppresses melatonin, the hormone associated with sleep.

2. BREAK YOUR FAST

Unless you're a full-time bodybuilder or graveyard shifter, you probably don't eat during the night. This means by the time you rub your bleary eyes in the morning, you've been fasting from food for 6-8 hours. Breakfast flips the metabolism back on like burners of a cold furnace, and I've found it a good time to get your sugar fix because it's quickly absorbed as glycogen and energy. You'll definitely find your metabolism will run hotter with a sugary breakfast upon awakening.

3. DRINK MORE WATER

Drinking plenty of water is the golden rule in dieting. We sometimes confuse thirst with hunger, so next time you feel "hungry", try drinking a glass of water. Water has a purifying effect, flushing out the food and toxins in your body and giving an energizing effect (not to mention sprinting to the bathroom can be great cardio).

4. NATURAL THERMOGENICS/STIMULANTS

There are a heck-ton of natural fat burners and digestive aids to choose from. Fat burning supplements like cayenne and guarana extract are proven energy-stokers, and I've found taking one apple cider vinegar tablet three times a

day will shed a few pounds in just a few weeks - even if you don't change anything else in your diet. Just don't live on them.

5. EAT SOME SUGAR

I can see some shouting "heresy!" and throwing down this book in disgust, but it's true. Sometimes you need a high glycemic, insulin-inducing uppercut of sugar to rattle the metabolism. It's common for professional bodybuilders to "cheat" with chocolate or ice creams while strict dieting for a competition, or even stop their diet to have a "high carb day". By cheating they (and you) are more likely to "win". However, if you're not working out at least three times a week, don't even look at that chocolate mint ice cream.

6. EAT SOME GOOD FATS

Partaking of unsaturated fats (and I'm talking fish and coconut oils) can increase energy, thermogenesis and positive hormonal activity which in turn burns fat. Fat burning fat. Ironic, no?

7. COLDNESS

According to test results conducted at the Thrombosis Research Institute in London, cold showers jumpstart the metabolism and increases oxygen circulation in the body. Eating cold food also increases the metabolism (the body must expend more energy warming digested food to body temperature), but in a much less significant way.

8. KELP AND SEAWEED

Bodybuilding legend Bill Pearl, on his popular and highly informative website *www.BillPearl.com*, informs the reader that sea vegetables Kelp and Dulse help maintain healthy

thyroid functions. He explains kelp supplements are also one of the best sources of minerals because billions of tons of topsoil are usurped by the ocean every year and Atlantic coast kelp is far richer in minerals than Pacific coast kelp.

9. EXERCISE

Take the stairs instead of the elevator. Drop to the floor right now and do twenty pushups. Go BASE jumping. You have options.

10. SIX SMALL MEALS A DAY

Eat all day long and lose weight – it sounds like a cheesy advert doesn't it? Well, it's also technically true. By eating six or more small meals a day every two to three hours, you can eat yourself thinner.

You Tube

Title: **Metabolism**

Tags: Weight Loss Fitness Working Out Eat Eating Fat Burning Slim Dieting Low Carbohydrate Obese Skinny fasting

From: BodyPerformanceTV

WATER RETENTION BLUES GETTING UNDER YOUR SKIN?

Rather than the weight scale, I suggest you rely on the appearance of your face and abs for indications of your progress. Variables like water retention and loss, glycogen stores, previous activities and what you just ate can confuse the weight scale and you. If you absolutely must use a weight scale, weigh yourself every third day, not every day, and always at the same time. You'll weigh the lightest in the morning, and typically get heavier as you eat and drink through the day. If you really want to drop some quick weight, drink water like a thirsty camel the day before (I'll explain soon).

Find a trustworthy mirror (have you noticed some mirrors are pathological liars?) and use it as your constant reference. Let's say for instance you glance in the mirror and your face is bloated, or the outline of your abs is smoothing out, it's time to make some changes. If it's because you've been carb-loading, it's time to "step off" and get back into ketosis. Start with a run around the block or shovel that old lady's walkway across the street.

Another reason for looking and feeling bloated could be too much sodium in your diet. The knee-jerk reaction would be to boycott all food and beverage and run and impromptu marathon (or surrender to a fate of fatness and go buy a bucket of chicken). However, first and foremost, you should drink copious amounts of the H2O. Remember: if you're feeling bloated, drink more water, not less. Hoarding is a survival mechanism the body employs when it's not getting enough water. By not drinking enough fluids (in particular water) and doing so only sporadically, you're inadvertently telling your body to store it away. And it will... in your face, your gut and anywhere else that will make you look heavier and toneless.

CHEMICALS YOU THOUGHT WERE SAFE

Like the Borg, there are foodstuffs that promise perfection but in reality are only health and weight problems waiting to assimilate with you... to become one with you and you with it! Don't become a mindless drone, trusting everything you eat and believing everything you read. You can prevent self-sabotage by staying away from these dangers:

THE ENEMY IS EVERYWHERE

The dark side of sugar and salt have long since been revealed, but there are two far more sinister additives lurking on your plate. Say hello to monosodium glutamate (MSG) and Aspartame. These "flavour enhancers" are found in countless foods and dietary supplements and studies conclusively show they cause obesity in laboratory animals as well as a shocking rap sheet of other health defects. Is it any wonder North America's rising rate of obesity coincides with the market saturation of these dangerous products?! Do yourself a favour, read ingredient listings on food labels and boycott products with MSG and aspartame (Sucrolose is evil too, so put the Splenda down). You'll save yourself unwanted weight and health problems.

SWEET AND SINISTER

Fruit juices and soda beverages are exactly the kind of hidden calories that pile up like bad debt. And then there is the sugar and fructose which cause further appetite and energy maladjustments. Avoid ingesting unnecessary calories and drink water. Unfortunately, even plain ole water can wreak havoc on your health and waistline. Next up... the shocking conclusion!

TERROR ON TAP?

We know water will help your stomach feel full, flush fat out of your system, clear your skin and keep the metabolism hustling. But did you know hard water is better for you than soft water? Hard water has a high mineral content (mainly calcium and magnesium in carbonate form, which the body requires in significant amounts) while soft water is stripped of the mineral content and has added sodium (something you may not need). In fact, cardiovascular mortality in men decreases as water hardness increases, as was shown in the county boroughs of England and Wales from 1961 and 1971. But while our drinking waters mineral content is generally A Good Thing™, fluoride in the water is not. Fluoride is a poison. It is biologically active even in the smallest doses and negatively affects hormonal and enzymatic activity in the body. If your water is treated with fluoride, use a filtering system or drink bottled water.

STAY AWAY FROM THESE FIVE INGREDIENTS

1. Trans Fats AKA hydrogenated and partially hydrogenated oils and shortenings

2. Artificial Sweeteners AKA Saccharin, Aspartame and Sucralose

3. Sugar Syrups AKA corn and maple syrup

4. Highly refined/bleached grains AKA white bread and pasta. *

5. Sugars AKA glucose and fructose.*

    * Exception: Can be taken immediately after a workout to replenish glycogen stores

Title: **Healthy Eating #10**

Tags: eating disorder healthy fat obese obesity monosodium glutamate MSG food additive

From: Urgelt

LOOK 10 LB THINNER BY TONIGHT!

You wake up and look in the mirror, only to find the corpulent countenance of a stranger staring back at you! Normally, you would ease the disappointment with some Nintendo and a bucket of bbq chicken wings, but you've got an important engagement tonight and want to look your best. So how do you look 10 lbs lighter in a single day?

Leg exercises. Quads are the biggest muscle group in the body and suck up a lot of caloric energy when in a state of repair. Squats in particular are a great way to work the quads and pretty much every other muscle in the body. I suggest pyramiding up in weight, starting light and lots of reps per set and as you add plates, lower the reps until you get down to six reps.

Here's how the exercise should be performed: Go all the way "down in the hole" until your glutamus maximus nearly touches the floor and come up slowly and in control. Ensure your movements are smooth, never jerky. Look straight forward, never face down, and watch the sweat pour off your face. Sweat is a key indicator you're creating a fat-burning environment. If sweat isn't pouring off your face, do squats until it does. A significant Growth Hormone response is also key to looking and feeling your best, so keep weight loads moderately heavy and the rest periods minimal (under 3 minutes and ideally only one minute). You'll be sore for a few days afterwards, but at least not during the engagement tonight. You'll have whipped your metabolism into hyper speed, your face will look thinner, and you'll feel "amped" from all the endorphins and other hormonal activity from such intense exercise.

EAT MORE AND GET SHREDDED?!

Bodybuilding pro and Mr.Olympia runner-up Keven Levrone says the secret to eating more and losing fat is to eat the "cleanest" foods you can while resistance training regularly. Weight training is the key to making your body an anabolic, metabolic freakazoid - provided it's at least thirty minute to one hour sessions, four to five times per week.

As for the nutritional part of the equation, your diet will consist of low glycemic, nutrient-dense fibrous complex carbohydrates and lean sources of protein, split up over six or more meals. You want to keep dietary fats off your plate as much as possible, with exception to one to three teaspoons of essential fats like flaxseed or hemp oil, taken preferably on an empty stomach. Count it as a meal if you'd like. Your caloric intake can be high however; you'll need the food to fund the extra development projects you've started. Follow this and watch your frame pack on lean muscle and shed body fat!

Here are some of the best protein and carbohydrate foods for this type of "diet".

CLEANEST PROTEIN SOURCES: Turkey, egg whites, sardines, herring, tuna, chicken, whey or soy powder

CLEANEST CARBOHYDRATE SOURCES: oatmeal, vegetables, fruits, yams, brown or wild rice.

CLEANEST OF BOTH: low-fat cottage cheese, fat-free yogurt, skim milk, pinto and red kidney beans

WHEN YOU'VE EATEN TOO MUCH

You really did it, didn't you? You ate the whole thing. While everyone else shied away from the carrot cake, all nestled snugly in a thick blanket of buttery vanilla icing, you had to unhinge your python jaw and swallow the entire cake. A single business card-sized piece is 5,000 calories, and there must've been a dozen servings. Instead, in a freakshow-ish display of gluttony, you reduced it to one.

Unless this is the initial salvo of a carb-load, such indulgence will do a number on the physique you worked so hard to create. You certainly don't want to go to sleep with so much food lying dormant in your stomach. So the plan now is damage control. It's even possible to come out ahead - gaining muscle instead of fat - if gone about in the right way.

Cardio isn't the answer when you can hardly move from the dinner table, let alone sprint five miles. Having personally been in this predicament, I've found the answer is resistance training. An hour or so after your meal, when the food in your belly has settled, hit the weights. Try working larger muscle groups like quads, chest, and back. Those muscles require more energy for recuperation than biceps or calves, thereby utilizing the food you've already eaten. That's the trick, put that food to use. Work out for an hour and skip any post-workout supplementation. You have enough calories loitering around your digestive tract to fund any repairs needed. Drink nothing but water until you go to bed. This not only keeps "traffic moving", but will help you stay satisfied and not back in the fridge. When you awake, you'll look and feel like the same able-bodied person you were before you made a greedy-gut of yourself at last night's dinner party.

BEST FOODS: MORNING AND NIGHT

Studies show your body needs and can process carbohydrates best in the morning. Here's why: by the time you wake up in the morning, your body has used up its carbohydrate reserves and likely in a catabolic state (when your body is deprived of protein and calories, it gleans much need amino acids from your muscles, making your muscles smaller). Don't allow this wanton destruction of heard-earned muscle to continue – now is the best time to eat carbohydrates (even the sugary stuff). It'll restock glycogen stores and halt catabolism in its tracks.

What about mealtime in the evening? Think low-glycemic. Think protein. Think fats. A chunk of cheddar cheese, a few poached eggs or a can of fish is a good choice for a late night snack. The digestive system processes fats better than carbohydrates at night, and fats and protein will provide the body with a steady stream of amino acids during your beauty sleep to prevent catabolism. As a free

bonus, sleep triggers hormonal activity key to health, in particular human growth hormone (hGH) which helps repair tissue, solidifies bones, tightens skin and even helps the body utilise the carbohydrate reserves we mentioned. But carbohydrates blunt hGH, so any sugar / carbohydrate / lactose (it's all high-glycemic to the body) consumption before bed will deprive you of a growth hormone response and surely be shuttled away into fat cells. Conclusion: It's best to eat carbohydrates in the morning and fats at night.

MASS HYSTERIA

THE CRISIS

Hollywood celebrities, men's magazine models, and other forces of mayhem plot to keep you small and weak - even normal! Meanwhile, it seems every other guy you look at has been weightlifting behind your back!

THE PLAN

Don't be caught unawares. With a steel bar, cold metal plates and this book as your secret weapon, you can escape the caustic grip of marginalization before it's too late!

WEIGHT LOWERING, NOT WEIGHT LIFTING

Just in case you're new to the "iron game", it's important to know that although it's referred to as "weight lifting"; it's the lowering of the weights that stimulates the most new muscle growth. Let's discuss what lifting and lowering are in physiological terms.

When one lifts a weight, the muscle shortens because the force of contraction is greater than the resistive force. It's known as a concentric muscle contraction. Visualize a dumbbell weight being lifted up on a bicep curl and you'll know what I mean. The lowering of the weight lengthens the muscle because the resistance is pulling away from the axis (that being the joint) and it's referred to as an eccentric muscle contraction, or a "negative". The tension on the muscle is greatest on the eccentric portion of the exercise, so naturally there will be more micro-tears in the muscle tissue. When the body heals these micro-tears, they will be bigger, stronger and more prepared for that same workload.

RAPPIN' 'BOUT REPS

The cool thing about resistance training (resistance training being an umbrella term for the two distinctly different pursuits of bodybuilding and weightlifting) is that it's a triple threat. It builds muscle, increases muscle strength and endurance, and burns fat simultaneously. There is simply no better way to get and stay fit. But you can't go off half-cocked, lifting weights willy nilly with no plan of attack. It helps to decide now what your primary goal is, because that will determine the right rep scheme to employ. For instance, if power is what you lust after, you're best off in the low rep range (three to eight reps per set - six being about right), and keep the set numbers low: three per exercise. If it's muscle mass you're after, stay within the 8 to 12 rep range, and anywhere from three to five sets. Also use this rep scheme if you're new to the iron game. If it's muscular endurance and more of a cardio workout, keep the reps up and the weight down. 12 to 20 (20 is a little on the extreme side, 15 reps per set is in "the zone"). Three to five sets per exercise within this high rep range should give you the entire workout you need to accrue the benefits of a cardiovascular exercise.

Here's the money line: Heavy weights and low reps keep the metabolism stoked the most after a workout, while low weights and high reps burn the most calories during a workout. Intensity should always be high.

Oh, and regardless of what you've read or heard, high reps schemes aren't any better at giving you a toned look than any other rep scheme. Rather, it's in the intensity you invest in each and every rep and not the volume perse. Besides, having a "toned look" means having a low body fat percentage. That will happen in due time.

Here's another way of determining how many reps you should do to build maximum muscle mass. Divide your body into upper and lower halves (please put down the saw). Anything above your abdominals and lower back (known as the core) is upper body. Upper body exercises should be within the 8-12 rep scheme, with 10 repetitions per set being ideal for mass building. Every muscle group below this median constitutes the lower body, and is worked most effectively with a higher rep range. Lower body exercises are generally most effective in the 15-30 rep range.

The reason being is you can't exhaust all the muscle fibers in the legs with only a few reps. You need to pound away at them with moderately heavy weights and higher reps to engage the many muscle fibers so densely packed in the thighs, hamstrings and calves. These muscles are often used and abused in everyday life, so a "shock" is required to encourage hypertrophy. Upper body parts on the other hand aren't as large or as exploited, so lower rep ranges are best.

If you're strength training and not bodybuilding for size, you'll want to keep the reps to no more than eight, regardless of whether it's upper or lower.

CALCULATE YOUR ONE REP MAX

Your one-rep max is the absolute maximum amount of weight you can lift without buckling under. You can determine this weighty number by mathematical means, ironically enough, and it's up to 99% accurate. Here's how it's done:

1.Choose a compound, multi-joint exercise.

2. Find a weight you can only do five reps of before your form begins to suck.

3. Once you've found that weight, punch that number into this formula if it's an upper body exercise like the bench press, military press or deadlift: (5RM x 1.1307) + .6998 or this formula if it's a lower body exercise like squats, the leg press etcetera:

(5RM x 1.09703) + 14.2546

Let's use a few examples. If you benchpressed 235lbs for 5 reps, shoehorn that number into the upper body formula like so: (235 x 1.1307) + .6998 which equals 266.4143. You can round it up to 270 lbs. Squatted 235lbs for five reps? Use the lower body formula: (235 x 1.09703) + 14.2546 = 272.05665 lb 1RM, but round it up to 275 lbs.

GET HARD, DENSE MUSCLES

When you enter the weight room of a local gym and scan the "competition" before getting busy, you can immediately tell who the heavy lifters are and who aren't. The heavy lifters have the bigger, denser muscles that give them a hard look so revered in bodybuilding culture. It's as if they've been forged from molten metal and sheathed with a layer of skin to dwell among mere mortals. They achieved that look of invincibility by utilizing power training techniques. Power Training consists of lifting weights so heavy, you can only do one to three reps per set in correct form. By lifting the absolute maximum weight you can muster, you stress the worked muscle fibers to their limit, making them thicker and bigger in what is called hypertrophy.

What's a good way to start? Have a "heavy day" when you train as heavy as you can using one of these three basic lifts: bench press, squat or deadlift. The military press is also considered a power lift, but should only be done as part of a power training program by weight lifters with at least 2 years experience. Let the involved muscle groups repair for a full week before training them again. Use 3 different exercises and go 1-3 reps in 3 sets.

Title: **BORN AGAIN CHRISTIAN BODYBUILDER RONNIE COLEMAN 800LBS**

Tags: JESUS   POWER

From: JESUSISLORDAMEN

TOP MUSCLE BUILDING EXERCISES IN THE UNIVERSE!

You want muscle, and you want it 10 minutes ago. No wasting time with lame exercises – you've got an appetite for construction and only the best mass builders known to man will suffice for you! So be it! Here's the top muscle building exercises for each muscle group:

Shoulders................................ military press

Triceps...................... close grip bench press

Biceps...................................... barbell curl

Forearms................... .wrist curl over a bench

Serratus.................................. ....rope pulls

Lats..................... underhand cable pulldown

Abdominals................................. crunches

Thighs.................................. front squats

Hamstrings................................. leg curls

Calves............................. seated calve raises

GLADIATOR IN TRAINING:

Gladiators would rub Allium cepa, bulb juice (Onion juice) on the skin to firm up muscles, and it's an ingredient still used today by health practitioners to relieve chronic joint and muscle pain, skin discolorations and counteract insect venoms.

TIME CRUNCH

You gotsta be nimble in this busy workaday world, especially when trying to squeeze a workout somewhere in between work, sleep and saving the planet from destruction. With only 20 minutes to devote to improving health and well-being, you can still have an effective workout which adds both resistance and cardiovascular elements. For example, do crunches between weightlifting sets. For example, between bench pressing sets, with no pause to rest, do crunches until your abs "hate your guts". This will add an aerobic component to your workout and tightens your abs, without wasting time moving from machine to machine. Similarly, train opposite muscle groups without rest. Gym rats and personal trainers often refer to this as compound sets, and they work like 90. Check out "The Dirty 30/30 Workout" for more compound crack pottery.

During a short workout, you'll want to employ as many muscles as you can, so you can have a residuary metabolic payoff that will last for the whole day or longer. Compound exercises like squats, dead lifts, chin ups and dumbbell or barbell lunges involve the whole body and recruit more muscles than bicep curls and other isolation movements.

THE DIRTY 30/30 WORKOUT

Work and life can be a major time suck, and can get in the way of developing and maintaining a super body. However, being pinched for time is the ideal time to bust out "plan B", aka the Dirty Thirties workout! The Dirty Thirties workout is designed for when you've only got 30 measly minutes to get it on and get it done (changing and showering included). Here's how it works:

Quickly pick two weight-bearing exercises for today. They should be all set up and ready to go. Imagine you jet into the gym and see both the bench press and the leg press available. Go to whatever is closest - in this case it's the bench press. Don't bother with stretching, just add a minimal amount of weight to the bar so you can safely and gentle pump blood into the pectorals. Do a set of 30 reps and without pausing to rest (you can do that when you die) then go to the leg press. Taking the same precautions for your legs, do an initial 30 reps warm-up with low weights. Continue going back and forth between work areas without pause, increasing the weight and pumping out exactly 30 reps per set at a blistering pace. Like a Chinese factory pumping out tchotchke, the Dirty Thirties workout is all about quantity, not quality. After 30 minutes, the Superman spit curl on your forehead will be soaked in sweat. By all rights, this should be one of the most intense workouts you've done in a long time, maybe ever!

You Tube   Title: **The "300" Movie Workout**

Tags: 300 Workout Exercise

29

SEVEN WAYS TO A RIGHTEOUS PUMP

For those of you not in the know, a "pump" is when the body part exercised becomes flushed with nutrient-rich blood. The muscle worked is warm and pliable under these prime conditions, and less prone to injury, even under the stress of heavy weights and shock tactics like forced reps. A pump is also anabolic, meaning it promotes muscle growth and constructive metabolism. You'll heal faster from an intense workout if you engorge the muscles in blood!

To some people, a good pump is a rare and lucky occurrence, and they consider it an unusually good workout (or just plain unusual) when it happens. However, it can and should be a regular "response" to weight training, especially if you're serious about building muscle. It's even a Weider training principle (called "Flushing") used by the top bodybuilding pros. Here's how to ensure a good pump, regardless of the muscle group worked:

1.   H20 AND BLOOD FLOW

Drink water regularly during your workout. Water drives the blood through the muscles. After each set, drink a modest amount of water (4 oz or so is enough) and hit the weights again.

2.   SKYLARKING STRICTLY PROHIBITED

Maintain a brisk tempo, as you want to keep your muscles warm and coaxing blood with every rep. Avoid lollygagging, skylarking, horseplay or any manner of tomfoolery which may lower your heart rate and allow the muscle to get cold.

3.   TAKE VITAMIN B3

Niacin, a B vitamin essential for a healthy nervous system and gastrointestinal tract, also tends to volumize blood in a big way. Take a 200 mg dosage with repeated trips to the water fountain to jam your muscles full of red fluid.

4.   DOWN DESICCATED LIVER TABLETS

Take 2-6 Desiccated Liver Tablets tablets with water, before and even during resistance training to get a monster pump. Desiccated Liver Tablets supply a quick hit of protein and produce healthy red blood cells.

5.   LIGHTER WEIGHTS, MORE REPS

The sustained pumping action of non-stop reps will guarantee your muscles will be engorged in nutrient-rich blood. Go four sets, 12-15 reps or more.

6.   USE MACHINES

Work the muscle directly. When you can eliminate the involvement of secondary muscles and extraneous movement and focus wholly on the muscle(s) being worked, more blood can flow there.

7.   DRINK A WORKOUT BEVY

Drink a sugary beverage with dissolved creatine. The sugar will raise your insulin level and drive the creatine into the muscle as you attack it set after set. I've experienced sustained pumps while sipping a protein and creatine beverage during my workout, and it's anabolic as heck. The sugar rush will also give you staying power and strength you might not have on an empty stomach.

VAUNTING VASCULARITY

Chicks love vascularity on a guy. They won't admit it, and they'll even mutter "ewww" as if gazing upon a squished bug - but make no mistake - deep down the women dig it. And why not, it's hardcore to look highly defined. On the macho-meter, vascularity is a nine-and-a-half out of a possible 10!

Now, if you're wondering how to achieve the same shredded-to-the-bone vascular look pro bodybuilders have during competition, you 1) need a low body fat percentage below a dozen and 2) awesome blood flow to the working muscles. Assuming you got number one locked down, there are a couple of supplements that will safely swell blood vessels: Desiccated Liver Tablets, Glycerol and Niacin. Desiccated Liver tablets were at one time a staple supplement with hardcore, old school bodybuilders. They are pure protein and can be taken liberally. They are good for you and create an awesome pump. Glycerol is fine too because it helps prevent dehydration by holding water in muscle cells. You can find glycerol in sports drinks and even those marshmallow candies that melt in your mouth (it may be called glycerin in the ingredients listing). Glycerol has a more subdued effect, but it's noticeable.

Niacin however can be toxic at high dosages, so the advice I was given (by the gym rat who told me about Niacin) was to stay within 200mg. I found when taking Niacin, my face turned red like a ripe hothouse tomato and my scalp tingled. This a) redness and b) tingling is thanks to the a) "flushing" effect of increased blood flow close to the skin and b) cells in the body releasing toxins, thereby producing a biologically active substance called "histamine" which is normally associated with allergic reactions. The symptoms are temporary and no cause for alarm (typically lasting 15 minutes or so).

As for niacin's effectiveness at increasing blood flow? The first time I used it was when doing biceps, triceps and forearms, and the pump was so incredible I thought the bulging veins in my biceps would burst! Even my forearms became wood hard and my workout had to be cut short. It worked too well! But let it be known: repeated overdosing can be a health risk, especially to the liver, so use sparingly. Of course it goes without saying to consult your doctor before implementing any information within this book.

FIVE HACKS TO BIGGER BICEPS

More and bigger are usually symptoms of greed and excessiveness. It can be perceived as a weakness, a lacking or deficit in the most ironic sense. But that doesn't apply to biceps. Bigger is better, and don't let anyone convince you otherwise! So go ahead and be greedy! Read these cool insider tips I've gleaned from experience and experts, grab a weight, and have at it!

1. UNILATERAL AND ULTRA-STRICT

Unilateral and ultra-strict form: if you're not harnessing the awesome power of the two U's, you're not growing like you could. Unilateral training (the strategy of working one limb at a time, and is often used to address a deficiency on one side) may even be more effective at stimulating muscle growth than bilateral training.

We all have a dominant side, be it our right or left. Unilateral training prevents our stronger side from compensating for our weaker side and hiding the imbalance. You can unleash all your strength and spoon-bending mental powers on the one limb for more hypertrophy.

Tip: If your form breaks anytime during the set, stop immediately and switch to a lighter weight. Using sloppy form to complete a rep is referred to as "cheating" and is a tactic to be used only by people with gargantuan muscles wearing spandex.

2. SQUEEZE

Squeeze the handle of the weight with a white-knuckled death grip on every rep, and on every contraction squeeze the muscle as hard as you can: that was the sage advice proffered by a veteran of the iron game and who had shoulders like boulders. And the old guy was onto something. The harder you contract the muscle, the more micro-tears are created in the muscle tissue (which equates to bigger muscles). And that lactic burn searing up your arm with every rep? This is a Good Thing®, according to a study done at the Center for Sports Medicine, Pennsylvania State University. Lactic acid appears to be a trigger for a growth hormone response (the ultimate anabolic biochemical of the human body), so grit your teeth and work through it!

For an amazing lactic acid burnfest, try this: After the last rep on every set of incline bench bicep curls, hang your arms to the side while continuing to grip the dumbbells for 30 seconds. Now that's a fire!

3. MIND-MUSCLE CONNECTION

Mind your own business, and your business is to visualize the biceps brachialis erupting like a mountain. It's called the mind-muscle connection and it's an essential ingredient to successful bodybuilding. Whether it's building a massive edifice like the Toronto CN tower or a bicep peak, you've got to see it in your mind's eye if it's ever going to be a reality. So when doing concentration curls, *concentrate and create!*

4.   ORDER UP A DOUBLE DOUBLE

Instead of a single post-workout bevy (with creatine natch), take two workout drinks: one before training and one after. As for training, biceps heal quickly and can be trained twice a week, so if you blast them on Tuesday, by Friday they should be ready for another rogering.

5.   BIGGER ARMS? WORK THE LEGS

Working the legs affect the central nervous system like no other muscle group because they are the biggest and strongest muscles in the body. The anabolic effect of blasting the *quadriceps femoris* is so significant; it benefits other muscles in the body including biceps. Don't ignore your "wheels" if you want big "pipes".

FIVE "TIPS" TO BUILDING A BICEP PEAK

It's good to have big arms, but how does one achieve a bicep with character and a craggy peak that stands out? It's not just a matter of genetics. You can coax out a hard jagged look only bodybuilding pros seem to know how to get - until now!

1.   ALTERNATE DUMBBELL CURLS

You can do these standing or sitting. IFBB sensation Richard "Magic Man" Jones says the key to building peaks is twisting the dumbbell near the top of the movement, when contracting the bicep muscle (and the trick works like a "beaut"). Start the exercise as normal, with the dumbbells in your hand facing your body, and as you bring the weight up you supinate the hand so that the pinkie finger faces towards you. Squeeze the muscle at the top of the movement and lower the weight slowly. Try three sets of 10 reps.

2. DOUBLE BICEP CABLE CURLS

Try this next time you're at the cable machine. Grab a handle in each hand and flex your biceps as if doing a double bicep pose. Focus on the contracting muscle, especially at the end of the movement. Now straighten out the arms again, slowly, feeling the continuous tension on the bicep. Again do three sets of 10 reps in strict form. Adjust the weight accordingly if you can do any more or any less repetition.

3. WEIDER PRINCIPLES WORK!

Employing Weider Principles like descending sets (google-fu the "Oxford method" for more information), forced reps (use sparingly) and rest-pause (10-15 second rest between each rep... that's right, *each rep*) will only help further the cause, provided you are getting adequate rest and your diet is sound.

4. FLEX MUSCLES HARD

Arnold Schwarzenegger was big on flexing his worked muscles as hard as he could after each set for 10 seconds or longer, and he had the steepest biceps ever in bodybuilding history.

5. VISUALIZE THE MUSCLE GROWING

Last but not least (and another tactic The Oak did) is to isolate the brachialis in your mind and imagine it as continental plates colliding and the rock buckling into the creation of a mountain! Hey, it worked for Arnold!

In conclusion, these bicep peaks aren't going to appear overnight, but as you faithfully include these exercises in your bicep workouts, you will notice a change in shape and overall height as I have.

You Tube

Title: **Ronnie Coleman Bicep work out with tips**

Tags: Ronnie Coleman Bodybuilding

From: nitostyle

SCULPT YOUR CHEST MUSCLES

To bring out the most favorable size and shape possible in the pectorals, you need to look at your chest as four distinct regions. They are Lower, Upper, Inner and Outer chest. Now, in reality they're not completely separate from each other - you can't work one region without affecting the other regions - but by using specific exercises you can target weak areas to get a fuller, more complete chest.

LOWER CHEST is easiest to target, and that would be why more people have over-developed lower pectorals and lagging upper pectorals. The classic bench press, flat bench flyes/presses and decline flyes/presses all attack the lower chest region. Dips should also be included in your workout routine, and may cultivate the "cut" underneath the nipple (although sheer muscle mass alone will achieve that look).

UPPER CHEST is coming more into awareness for most bodybuilders. I think it's because the pros have been driving the point home in the bodybuilding magazines the past few years. To target this area, do copious amounts of incline presses and flyes. If your hands are raised straight ahead of you, cable crossovers can affect this area, but more so the inner region. Provided body fat levels are in check, developed upper pectorals will give you some striations when you do a most muscular pose.

INNER CHEST development requires focus and intense muscle squeezing unlike any other body part. The best exercises for this area are pec-deck flyes and bent-over cable crossovers, with your chest parallel to the floor. Flat bench and decline bench dumbbell presses can also build the inner pectorals when you use explode up through the lift and squeeze your chest together with your upper arms at the top of the movement. Hold the squeeze as hard as you can for two seconds then release and lower your arms to finish the rep.

OUTER CHEST is worked with a wide grip bench press, as well as flat and incline dumbbell flyes.

You Tube

Title: **Flex Magazine Workout - Chest**

Tags: BodyBuilding   BodyBuilder   Flex   Workout   Muscle   Chest

From: KaitoChan

SINGLE BEST WAY TO STIMULATE MUSCLE GROWTH

The best, most efficient way to build big muscles - bar none - is by going as heavy as you can for one to three reps, first thing in your workout. By exerting the maximum amount of initial tension on the muscle, more muscle fibers will be engaged during flexion. More contracting muscle fibers during your workout result in more muscle mass. Fitness experts and personal trainers know this training system as *high-intensity, low volume* training, and bodybuilder forefathers Mike Mentzer and Dorian Yates (among others) "championed" this system with great success.

High Intensity, Low Volume has other advantages of other rep schemes and training regimes. It dramatically reduces the chances of overtraining, (a common problem for enthusiastic newcomers), and lifting your three rep max "wakes up" your nervous system so slightly lower weights that would have been a challenge before will seem easier (see "Psyche Out Your Nervous System" for more gory details). You'll be able to do more reps with higher weights which again, result in more muscle mass. Fully stretch before attempting this shock tactic, have a spotter when necessary and do it on occasion, not everyday.

FIVE WAYS TO UTTERLY DESTROY PLATEAUS

Muscle plateaus can be a demoralizing experience, especially when you feel your doing everything within reason (and within the boundaries of the law). You bump up your calories and take a creatine-laden post workout drink immediately after resistance training. You hammer away at the slacker body part with heavy weights set after set and week after week and... nada. Zip. Nothin' doing. Even routines advocated by top bodybuilding pros do nothing to break the plateau. You wonder if steroids are a solution, but they're not. There's fair and square, all-natural ways of breaking through.

1) First, an anecdote: My biceps had halted growing for

39

almost a year, and I was on the verge of defeat. I had pounded my biceps into oblivion every week and still got no love. Then, while researching natural growth hormone response, I happened across a new arm exercise called the spider curl. I made a mental note of it and tried it out next day in the gym. Man did it make my biceps sore, for nearly a week! For the first time in a long time I had hope. Moral of the story? Try some new exercises and strive to get sore!

2) Train the body-part twice a week. This really makes a difference, especially with arms. You need to hit the body-part hard, once at the beginning of the week when your strength is best, and then three-quarters through the week to remind it whose boss.

3) I heard somewhere that when you start weightlifting, it's like hiring a bricklayer. And what does that bricklayer need to stay busy working? Big cinder blocks. In this case, cinder blocks are protein. Eat plenty of protein (at least 1oz per pound of body weight), and preferably from different sources. Whey protein is best, but eggs, chicken and lean cuts of red meat are also excellent. Buy some protein bars (you can get them cheap when close to the expiration date) and take them with you wherever you go.

4) Eat at night. Especially if you're sore, you need to eat around the clock. Keep those bricklayers working 24/7. You're trying to force the issue with that plateaued body-part. Don't give it any excuse not to grow.

5) It could be that you're working too hard in the gym, too often. You need resting time for your body to recuperate and grow. If you're spending anymore than five days a week in the gym, you need to get a life. Better yet, lose your life in the service of others. The

signature of a true superhero!

DON'T BE A WORKING STIFF: 10 WAYS TO AVOID POST-WORKOUT SORENESS

Stiffness and soreness 24-48 hours after a workout usually means you've stimulated muscle growth. This is good, and it's commonly referred to as *Delayed Onset Muscle Soreness,* or DOMS for short. If, however, the pain or soreness occurs during or immediately after training, is an indication your muscles aren't getting enough blood and oxygen. This is bad. This condition is known as *ischemia* or *Acute Onset Muscle Soreness.* Despite the name, there's nothing "cute" about it (laugh people, it's a joke) because trained muscles are having a hard time disposing of metabolic waste (primarily lactic acid). This leads to an inevitable lactic acid build-up and soreness will ensue.

Regardless of whether it's *Acute Onset Muscle Soreness* or DOMS, there's no need to renounce physical activity forever. Use these helpful hacks to minimize the discomfort after a good hardcore training session.

1. INCREASE PROTEIN

Absolutely most important when your body's on the mend is to make sure you're eating enough protein. Protein supplies the body with the building blocks (called amino acids) so it can rebuild the muscle bigger, better, faster... you get the idea. Whey protein is superior, but any form is suitable provided you take an amino acid supplement to ensure the protein goes to work right away. Eat at regular intervals, even at night until the muscle recoups.

2. EAT CARBS

It's no time to be on a low carb diet. You need to restock those muscle glycogen stores and keep them stocked until

41

the muscle tissue is healed. Full glycogen stores will lessen the ache, speed healing and give the muscle strength when recruited for daily activities. Your best sources for glycogen are whole grain foods including brown rice, oats, whole wheat bread and barley.

3. BOOST CREATINE AND GLUTAMINE INTAKE

Ingest double the amount you regularly take of creatine and glutamine in a sugary, insulin-inducing beverage to drive those amino acids into the muscle. This'll hasten the healing process, along with all the other benefits associated with these non-essential amino acids.

4. GLUTAMINE, CREATINE AND A NANNER

Want a supplement that'll help you heal fast? Glutamine is the flea's eyebrows for quick recovery from workouts. Add 5 mg along with 5 mg creatine to your post-workout beverage and blend in a banana for the healing properties of potassium.

5. IT'S A STRETCH BUT...

A study from the University of Tampa, Tampa, Florida suggests stretching during sets and immediately after resistance training can make a small difference in the intensity and duration of your stiffness and soreness, while stretching before resistance training does "squat". A warm-up jog beforehand may also stave off soreness because it ensures adequate blood supply to the working muscles. Afterwards, a sure-fire way to flush out lactic acid after a leg workout is to cycle for a half hour to 45 minutes.

6. SLEEP

If you have the luxury of napping after a workout, do so. The human body repairs quicker and more efficiently when asleep (human growth hormone release is partly responsible for the accelerated recovery). As for retiring to your sensory deprivation chamber for the evening (you have one, don't you?), some may need six hours and some will need more than eight, but if you need to be awoken by an alarm clock, you're not getting enough shuteye.

7. IF YOU MUST TAKE A PAINKILLER...

Don't take ibuprofen (aka Advil) if packing on maximum muscle mass are important to you. A trial published in the Journal of Clinical Endocrinology and Metabolism suggests the painkiller ibuprofen may undercut your gains. Besides, it's primarily an anti-inflammatory, not a pain killer, so it won't ease your stiffness and soreness after leg day anyway. Aspirin is your man.

8. BREAKUP WORKOUTS TO 2 OR 3 DAYS

Legendary bodybuilder Dorian Yates has proven training a muscle group once a week is enough – provided you train like a mad fiend. Instead, try not going so hard, but rather work on the same body-part twice or even three times in a week instead. Top athletes employ this workout strategy so they can perform in their sport during the week without being hindered by Delayed Onset Muscle Soreness (DOMS). You could even confine working a particularly problematic body part to one set a day, every day of the week. It works to build muscle, but with no soreness!

9. C + E BEFORE/VITAMIN COCKTAIL

A study published in the European Journal of Applied Physiology suggests taking vitamin C and E (known antioxidants) before a workout will decrease muscle soreness, and it's an effective free radical scavenger that synergises well with vitamin E and Selenium. Toss in a multi to boot and you have a great post-workout vitamin combo.

10. WORTH A TRY

This may be old school coach folklore, but rumour is if you spend 15 minutes in the sauna room and take a cold shower immediately thereafter, soreness in the legs will be reduced significantly.

SUCCESS WITH FAILURE

Cajole a stubborn muscle into growing by taking every set of a particular exercise to failure (failure means being unable to execute another rep with good form). Pick a weight, not too heavy, and bang out as many reps as you can using perfect form. It may be up to 50 reps or even more. The second set you do will likely be much less weight, but be sure to go to failure again. Continue this until you can only eek out 5 reps before big salty crocodile tears roll down your face and your worked muscles submit to failure. It really works good, and it really hurts good.

Not everybody is a fan of failure however. According to ExRx Exercise and Muscle Directory (*www.exrx.net*), Mr. Olympia and strongman Franco Columbo denounced the use of failure in an article in wrote in the 1980's, and even Russian Kettlebell champ Pavel Tsatsouline has said those who claim failure can make you stronger are full of Bolshevik.

Here's what I know: going to failure is awesome for stimulating muscle growth, but if used too frequently, it can be brutal on the nervous system and may even hamper strength gains. Here's why: repeatedly forcing reps activates a proprioceptive sensory receptor organ called the *neurotendinous spindle*, which inhibits muscular contraction to prevent the muscle from possible injury, and are two well-known strongmen who oppose the use of forced reps.

THE REVERSE PRE-EXHAUST TACTIC

If there's a tenaciously unwilling body part that refuses to grow, try reverse pre-exhausting. What you're doing with this method is fatiguing all the supporting muscles that may help you work a certain muscle group, which in turn forces the primary muscle being targeted to do all the work lifting the weight.

Take for instance barbell curls for the biceps. Do you find your front (anterior) deltoids always getting involved, no matter how you try to tighten up your form? If so, blast your anterior deltoids until they're weak as newborn kittens, *and then* do barbell curls with the weight you're accustomed to. You'll be forced to resort to good form and engage all the muscle fibers of your biceps. Your other alternative is to drop to weight and lift something a little more realistic.

Another example may be your upper pectorals. If you find them lacking, don't put them at the front of your routine, put them last. After you've pummelled your lower and mid pectorals to utter exhaustion, now do upper chest and notice how much more those specific muscles need to work!

COOL AS ICE HEALING

After mercilessly slamming muscles for an hour, you need to recuperate in a timely manner. Try icing the worked muscle group for 20-30 minutes while stretching. Ice hastens blood flow to the muscle, thereby accelerating recovery, in a process known as *reactive hyperemia*. It's effective for alleviating soreness and cooling any lactate burn still lingering. Keep a couple of bags of ice in the freezer for next leg day, or freeze Dixie cups filled with water and use them as ice holders!

'PECTACULAR PECS

Maybe a chest you could sit a martini glass on is not in the cards for most of us (not without chemical coercion anyway), but you can make the most out of your genetics by earnestly applying these choice chest constructors to your next pec day.

PRE-EXHAUSTION

This one works beauty. Start with dumbbell presses, first with light weights and with reps as high as 20, then pyramid down until you're as heavy as you can go doing 6 reps in perfect form. Do at least three of these sets, preferably until supporting muscles like anterior deltoids and triceps are exhausted. Your chest won't be exhausted however. It's a much larger muscle and it can go a few more rounds still, so following up with the bench press will force more of the workload on the chest (because said supporting muscles are already fatigued), thereby causing more muscle stimulation.

MACHINES

Machines are effective because they're designed to focus the brunt of the weight to the primary muscles (chest) and all but exclude secondary muscles (triceps). On a machine like the hammer smith machine you should feel stress on the pectorals from start to finish. 100% of your force and focus can go to attacking the pecs and the energy won't be displaced trying to stabilizing the weight. One more thing: change your grip on the handles often. By simply moving your hands to different spots on the handles, you can hit the working muscles differently.

STRESS THE NEGATIVE

Let's use the classic bench press for illustration. Push the barbell up quickly (albeit under complete control) and squeeze the muscle at the top of the movement for a second. Keep a slight bend in the elbows, never "locking out" (meaning straightening your arms and locking your joints). Now lower the weight, s-l-o-w-l-y for a count of four. Notice a greater burn in your "pectaculars" and more sore later the next day, which is signaling new growth.

FLEX THE PEX

After every set, clasp your hands in a most muscular pose and squeeze the pec muscles together with all you can muster for 30 seconds. You'll feel warm blood charge into your chest and create an anabolic pump you'll feel for an hour after you leave the gym. Even better, it'll stimulate more growth, faster!

NARROW IS THE ROAD

When doing dumbbell presses and flyes, don't lower the weights below the proudest part of your pectorals. Some do it for that "deep stretch", but in reality it's increasing the chance of shoulder injury and it's not working the chest. Keep the dumbbells within eyeshot at all times, and never go below parallel to ensure you're working the chest and not the anterior deltoids. And another thing, the wider your grip, the more you stretch your deltoids and outer chest.

DON'T WASTE YOUR TIME

Not all exercises are alike and equal. Some exercises have only one purpose, and that is to burn fat, while other exercises are great for adding new muscle. Cable cross-over are good at neither. Rather, they're an ideal exercise for toning and shaping and for the occasional warm-up before bench pressing. So if you wanted a big muscular chest, like yesterday, don't bother doing them. Save your time and energy for mass building exercises like bench presses and flyes (incline, flat and decline in that order), dips and machines.

SUPER SLOW TRAINING (SST)

Super Slow Training (SST) generated a serious buzz awhile back, with it's tardily tempo and promises of supernal strength and muscle mass, which were backed by scientific study. The excitement has since been tempered by similar studies which have actually refuted those claims of the SST camp, but it's worth a shot for Bobby Newcomer who's learning the iron game for the first time.

Traditional SST employs a whopping 10 second concentric movement (i.e.: lifting the automobile) and a four second eccentric (or lowering) motion, which effectively stops momentum dead in its tracks. This is good for two apparent reasons: less momentum means the muscle is under greater tension, ergo, more muscle fibers are recruited resulting in greater muscle stimulation and hypertrophy. In fact, SST training protocol encourages training no more than one set in super slow mode a week, due to the massive micro-trauma created in the muscle tissue. And peep this out: super slow reps taken to failure stimulate both slow and fast twitch muscle fibers. You can see how quelling momentum is the crux of SST's scientific studies.

The second reason less momentum equals more results is less momentum permits greater control of the weight, which decreases the likelihood of injury most common with noobs and allows greater focus on the worked muscle.

There are plenty of derivations on SST training which improve its effectiveness. For example, pro bodybuilders are known to place equal time on the "down phase" (eccentric portion of the movement) as the concentric phase, because as you and I both know, a slow and controlled eccentric phase is where you build the most muscle. Heck, it may be even better to shorten the concentric phase anywhere from two to four seconds (which will allow you to lift more weight) and only elongate the eccentric side of things. Try it out, experiment, and when it makes your muscles burn so bad you wish mommy was there to hold your widdle hand, then you've got an effective formula for you.

A couple of caveats: super slow lifting demands high intensity and the mental focus of Charles Xavier. Don't even bother if you're not 100% mentally and physically charged. Also, while super slow training can make you strong and look strong (with a little tweaking), it's only appropriate for larger muscle groups like legs, chest and shoulders using compound exercises. Compound movements for legs include leg press or hack squats, for shoulders: the shoulder machine and the machine press for the pectorals.

DIAMOND-SHAPED CALVES ARE FOREVER

Ever noticed the angular cuts of top bodybuilders' calves? They have what are referred to as diamond-shaped calves because they're so sharply defined they can slice glass in half. These diamond-shaped calves cannot be bought in stores, and you can't give them as a gift at Christmas time in front of a romantic fireplace. They must be wrought by untold pounds of pressure and unearthed by digging deep down from within one's will.

Listen up: when doing calve raises, point your toes inward and squeeze the gastrocnemius muscle hard at the top of the movement (when on the balls of your feet and calves are fully extended). Hold for two seconds and lower your heels slowly to below parallel. By consciously contracting the muscle as described, and using the mind-muscle connection technique, you can accentuate the inner portion of the calves, giving you the same angular look that is a girl's best friend ;)

You Tube   Title: **Calf Raise**

Tags: legs fitness exercise weightlifting

From: johnspencerellis

MEGA LIFTS BURNS MEGA FAT

Recent scientific findings have shown one's metabolic rate is increased more, and for a longer period of time after the workout, when intense heavy weightlifting in the 6-8 rep range is employed rather than lighter weights and higher reps. Even with longer rest periods, lifting heavy revs the metabolism hotter and longer than high rep schemes. Also consider you're more likely to actually build muscle with heavier weights you can only squeeze eight reps out of.

The key to immobilizing fat and building muscle with resistance training is to rattle the nervous system's cage a bit. Challenge yourself. Be intense. The rewards are far greater

PSYCHE-OUT THE NERVOUS SYSTEM

An effective method for boosting your lifting strength is with nervous system trickery called "Enhanced Neural Drive". The principle is this: when you lift your one rep max (1RM) on a multi-joint exercise like bench press or squat, you amp up the central nervous system so on subsequent lifts you can lift more weight than usual. It psyches the nervous system into thinking another super-heavy set is ahead, and it will call in more muscle fibers to do the job. Hormones like adrenaline and testosterone will kick into full effect after a heavy first lift. This is when you move down to a slightly "heavier than usual" weight for whatever rep scheme you're currently employing. Try 10-20% more weight for starters and adjust accordingly as you become more comfortable with this tactic. You'll notice the next set will appear lighter, even if it's normally quite heavy for you!

Now, some words of caution: use the Enhanced Neural Drive sparing. Never do a 1rep max on small muscle groups like calves, abs, traps or forearms, and it's not meant for isolation movements like lateral raises, flyes or leg extensions. This tactic works best with exercises where many stabilizing and antagonist muscles come into play, primarily the big four mass builders: squats, deadlifts, bench press and military press. You should also have at least two years gym experience before trying this or any other advanced technique. Why? Because you need to know good form and a decent level of musculature you you'll just end up getting hurt!

SWEATIN' OUT THE TOXINS

The composition of a single drop of sweat is an incredible biochemical grocery list: salt, lactic acid (a harmless waste product of worked muscles), uric acid, ammonia, fat molecules, vitamin c and the remaining 99% being water. But did you know sweating is also a detoxification mechanism for the body? It's estimated 30% of all the crap in our system is expelled via perspiration, which is significant considering the arsenic, heavy metals, particles, gases and naturally produced toxins from protein metabolism that accumulate in our bodies. And these toxins are everywhere, in our air, the food we eat, and hiding in our prescription medications, hand soaps and shampoos. When accumulated, these poisons can lead to symptoms ranging from fatigue to headaches, sluggish metabolism, poor digestion and even heart disease and cancer. Sweating is by far the most accessible and passive method of liberating poisons from our body.

The easiest way to trigger a good outpouring of the skin pores is in a sauna. A good session in the hotbox will serve to clear the skin and purge the body of impurities (albeit sweat can't take all the props, kidneys and the liver are the body's main detoxifiers and do significantly more work). Regular exercise is the other obvious way of detoxification.

SEARING SEPARATION INTO QUADS

You've been grinding it out at the squat rack week after week for years now, and you want your chevrolegs to show for all the sweat, tears and puke you put into it. To get thighs with the size and separation of Captain Canuck, it's time to switch it up! Bone up on the same tactics pro bodybuilders and our hero from the north use:

DEVELOP ALL FOUR THIGH MUSCLES

Quad means four, and there are four muscles that make up the muscle group. They are the *rectus femoris* (front), *vastus intermedius* (front), *vastus lateralis* (outer) and the *vastus medialis* (inner).

For the highly noticeable V-shape delineation in the middle of the thighs, work the rectus femoris and vastus intermedius with the tried and true squat and leg press. Leg extensions are also very effective, and a good warm-up and finishing-off exercise on leg day.

A pronounced tear drop muscle (which is above the knee cap on the inside of the thigh called the vastus medialis) is extremely impressive and shows you're no stranger to front squats. Keep a wide foot stance and your toes pointed outward when doing this squat variation. Lunges are also very effective and should be included often.

Front squats, leg presses and hack squats will develop the outer quads with time and diligence.

BLOCK THAT CHICK HORMONE

Reducing persistent fat on the thighs may be as easy as eating soy. Soy products contain phytoestrogens, a natural compound which acts as an estrogen blocker. Why an estrogen blocker? Because when testosterone levels are high, the body will convert some of this alpha male muscle-building hormone to the female hormone called estrogen in a natural process called aromatization. Estrogen causes excess water retention and fat storage, and in the usual problematic areas for women - the hips and thighs.

BLOW UP THOSE THIGHS

Explosive plyometric moves will bring definition, size and strength to those thighs. Try exercises like the football drill (run as quickly as you can in one spot for 30 seconds, shifting your bodyweight from side to side like a running back, then drop down and do a push up spring back up into sprint mode again), running stairs and skipping.

GET DOWN... ALL THE WAY DOWN

Bodybuilding legend Tom Platz was quoted as saying: ""Half-Squats will give you half-legs", and who's to argue with the man with the biggest and best legs ever in the business? All the top bodybuilding pros do full squats,

meaning they go beyond parallel so their rump touches their ankles. It stimulates more muscle fibers and the strength improvements over "half-squats" are substantial, but you won't be able to do as much weight.

TEAR IT UP

It's a good strategy never to get over 10-15% body fat anyway, but if you want highly defined legs, it's mandatory to stay lean. Fat tends to stubbornly stick around in those nether regions, so taking a dual-pronged approach like cycling is a good idea. Studies have shown (as if we even needed studies for this) cycling stimulates muscle growth and burns fat and it's a safe form of cardio (safer than running) for heart patients or people with high blood pressure. So strap on a helmet and hit the road Jack!

FLEX THE QUADS BETWEEN SETS

During leg exercises, Arnold Schwarzenegger flexed and squeezed his thighs between every set, creating the deep separation and striations that set a new standard in bodybuilding. Flexing helps bring out more definition and a harder look, and over time, the overall quality of the muscle will be better.

Title: **bodybuilding exercise: lunges, a great whole leg workout**

Tags: bodybuilding bodybuilder leg quad hamstring exercise lunges home workout

From: scooby1961

"PUMP UP" MUSCLES AN INCH BIGGER – IN ONE DAY

Proportion is critical for the serious bodybuilder who strives for a symmetrical and streamlined physique. Those who focus too much on a few favorite bodyparts and forsake the rest of their body (yeah, I'm looking at you chicken legs) end up only cheating themselves and looking silly. Yet even the conscientious and thorough citizens among, those of us who work every muscle duteously, still have bodyparts that refuse to cooperate. Calves are mine. Professional bodybuilders and Superhero's have theirs. Everybody does.

So what's the solution to this injustice? The long term and more permanent solution is to commit extra time and energy into developing the muscle, just as you would a wayward child. A tactic I've had work for me is to do one set of the same exercise, five days a week, for three weeks straight. I did one set of leg extensions at the end of my regular workout to beef up my quads, and after only a week I noticed an improvement.

There is an even quicker way. This method, pioneered by old-school bodybuilders of yore, adds up to an inch of size to a lagging muscle *the very day before a bodybuilding competition or day at the beach*. Here's what you do: The day before, do one set of 10 reps every hour for up to 14 hours and do nothing else (be sure to measure the muscle beforehand). Now measure the muscle afterwards and marvel at how your muscles are up to an inch bigger than normal!

GET GINORMOUS WITH FOOD

Workout all you like and does everything right, but if you're not eating enough quality calories in a day, you're not going to get more muscle. For those hard-gainers who have trouble downloading enough calories to install muscle, here are proven tricks to upgrading your appetite:

PROTEIN BARS: There was an ad in a bodybuilding magazine from a popular supplement company which had a full page photo of a guy's enormous freakish leg as he was doing squats. I was inspired, and I cut the picture out and taped it on my bedroom mirror to fuel my desire to have gnarly oak tree legs like him. The next few months I concentrated heavily on my leg workouts, and with that I bumped up my daily protein intake quite dramatically with the help of protein bars. Each bar contains upwards of 30 to 60 grams of protein, and you can likely by them by the box for cheap when close to expiry (as I did). As a result, I couldn't wear certain jeans because my thighs were too big. Goes to show, protein bars pack on muscle mass when eaten liberally.

You Tube

Title: **Protein Bars: DIY Gym Food**

Tags: food cooking diet fitness health healthy protein workout

From: mistertut

CHEW GUM: In high school, I used to have math class right before lunch. I recall one class I was chomping on a piece of gum and my teacher took issue with it - not for disrupting the other students with 'cow-chewing-it's-cud' sounds I was making, but for chewing gum on an empty stomach. He shook his head woefully in front of the whole class and said, "That's very cruel to your stomach, chewing gum when you're hungry." That stuck with me, and I've since avoided doing such a masochistic act, lest my math teacher's stern expression haunts me again. But it's true, besides fresh breath and clean teeth, chewing gum stimulates saliva production and activates digestive enzymes. You're gut will assimilate food faster so you can consume more calories. Chewing gum after meals may help protect against heartburn too.

EAT YOUR FAVE FOODS: Provided the food has some nutritional merit, go ahead and eat what you actually like to eat instead of bland bodybuilding mainstays like broccoli and sardines. Write a list of your favorite foods, or stroll down the isles of the local grocery store and pick out the foods you would normally restrain yourself with. You may be so caught up in eating "bodybuilding foods" that you have crushed your diet in the process. Live a little.

FRUIT YEA, GREEN VEGETABLES NEA

Hard-gainers want to eat fruit for the same reason dieters abstain from it: fructose tends to make people eat more. It's due to the suppression of leptin, the hormone responsible for feeling full. You'll also want to forgo the dark green vegetables. The fiber and high vitamin and nutrient content will keep you satiated for long periods of time, and make it more difficult for the hard gainer to intake enough calories. Opt for high glycemic, starchy vegetables like corn and potatoes. Goes to show: fruits are for building, vegetables are for cleansing.

GLADIATOR IN TRAINING:

Gladiators were generally stocky beefcakes because the extra weight protected them from potentially lethal deep wounds and gave them added strength and advantage over smaller opponents.

WEAKNESSES INTO STRENGTHS

There are certain nameless individuals (cough *chicken legs *cough) who have the tendency to pass the buck-buck-buck and avoid hard workouts in favor of easier exercises, but this would certainly not be you! You want a complete and balanced physique and let all your muscle groups taste the iron. But for those who'd rather run like a chicken than get in the trenches and battle for a better body, consider Mike Mentzer's Heavy Duty system. It's the one set workout Dorian Yate's used to prepare for and win the 1992 Mr. Olympia. You heard right! Merely one lonely set per muscle group, but at 100% maximum intensity. This means you'll be going to failure and beyond by using rest-pause or negative reps until you cry like a howler monkey.

The ACSM Weight Training Guidelines (1995) show performing more than one set of high intensity resistance exercise does not lead to significantly greater gains in muscular strength, endurance, or body composition. The Heavy Duty system is all you'll likely need to get the job done quickly.

One more word of advice: When you're feeling strongest, tackle the weak spots on your physique, and do the exercises you normally avoid.

USE THE TRI-FORCE

The triceps, as you may or may not know, is an important muscle we all heavily rely on for throwing basketballs from three point land. And in an effort to increase our collective shooting percentage, I'd like to share two (ahem) "pressing" matters regarding effectively working the triceps muscle.

The first important thing to remember about working out the triceps is positioning of the elbows. All else pales in importance, because if your not doing the exercises with proper form, your wasting valuable crime-fighting time and your triceps won't grow. Keep your elbows in and stationary during the entire movement. Let the triceps do the work and the arms act as levers. Stay focused and the movement strict, and soon your triceps muscles will have muscles!

The second important factoid is triceps press downs are one of the few exercises I know of where "locking out" is acceptable [*]. Locking out allows you to contract the triceps muscle hard for better hypertrophy, and injury isn't likely doing press downs since the weight is being pulled down as opposed to pressing down, and the stress can be immediately released. The lat pulldown and bicep curls also fit this description and can be safely locked out.

[*Locking out is straightened arms or legs while under the stress of bearing weight, and places the stress on the joint and connective tissue instead, which could lead to injury.*]

MANLY SHAPE AND SYMMETRY

What do superheros, bodybuilders and football players all have in common? Shoulders the size of boulders, my friend. Through-out the annals of time, broad shoulders taper and a comparatively small waist have been the representation of physical strength and alpha maleness. A dramatic v-taper strikes fear in the hearts of villains, brings yearning to the souls of women and instils awe in the minds of children.

The beauty is any man can imbue himself with bigger shoulders with consistent resistance training using mass-building exercises (as opposed to toning exercises which are more for fat burning and adding detail). The deltoids muscles cover the shoulder joint and are actually three-in-one, meaning there are three different heads to the muscle that allow the arm to move in so many ways. The three heads of the deltoid muscle are the anterior (front), medial (side) and posterior (back) and all three need to be trained and developed if you're to achieve big, bulbous shoulders. Seated military presses, dumbbell side laterals and barbell front raises should be your bread and butter for the front and side deltoids. To isolate the rear deltoids, try bent over cable laterals and incline bench lateral raises (lying face down). Start your workout with ample stretching and follow with a couple of light warm-up sets. Always use slow and deliberate movement, and focus not on the weight but on the contracting muscles.

Bodybuilding icon Shawn Ray has said the secret to symmetry is the full development of abs and calves. By narrowing your midsection and defining your abs through diet and exercise, you make all other muscles on your upper body look bigger, in particular your pecs. Consider that the abdominals are the "optical center" of the body. The eyes naturally rest on them first, so here are some tips to get your stomach looking like a washboard and not a load of laundry!

- Abs grow quickly, so don't work them year round. Doing so only makes your midsection thicker, ruining the v-taper effect.

- Properly training the abs requires flexion of the spinal cord. Focus on only spinal cord movement to get that "crunch" you need. Any so-called abs exercise that doesn't have the spinal cord flexion as the primary movement isn't properly working the abs.

- If you can perform 20 or more reps of any abs exercise, it's not building muscle!

[Generally speaking, body fat percentage of total body weight for a male should not exceed 15%, while a woman should not typically exceed 22% body fat. Delineation of the rectus abdominus muscles begin to show through the skin at 12% bodyfat or less.]

- No need for funky bizarre ab movements, the basics work fine.

- The "secret" to unveiling the full delineated rectus abdominus muscle is to do an *unreasonable* amount of intense cardio. Read into that whatever you want, but when you achieve the look you'll know what I mean.

- Hooking your feet under a solid object while doing sit ups don't work the abs. The hip flexors (primarily the iliopsoas) will do the work because the body takes the path of least resistance. Anytime a stronger muscle is given a chance to do the job, it will.

- Wear a weight belt when doing deadlifts and squats. Obliques are recruited more when not using a belt, whereas abs tend to take the brunt of pressure when a weight belt is used. As you may or may not know, developed obliques will widen your waist. However, don't let your lower back get atrophied either. Isolate those important muscles with hyperextensions and "good mornings" without the weight belt on.

- This may seem like a long shot, but if you're doing a lot of cycling, consider wearing a weight belt. Again, it's those darn obliques that like to get in the action and, while we don't want them to be atrophied, we don't want them hypertrophied either. Nonetheless, be rational if you're going to take this approach. If you experience shallow breathing or painful cramping, stop immediately.

- Developed glutes and quads will also give the illusion of a small midsection. The same idea holds true for calves. Shapely, muscular calves can give the illusion of bigger thighs and less-nobby knees.

RUN FOR YOUR LIFE

THE CRISIS

With obesity and other health problems creeping within the shadows of inertia and stress conspiring to take you down to an early grave, it's time to run... run for your life!

THE PLAN

This heart-pumping chapter reveals how to run longer, stronger and transform yourself into a healthier, happier supra-you along the way. There's a lot of exciting info here, and if it doesn't leave you gasping for breath, *you must be clinically dead!*

CARDIO-RESPIRATORY ENDURANCE: GET SOME

Cardio-respiratory endurance might be the most important single subject in this book. It is the oxygen-transporting capacity of the body, the cardiac output of the heart (stroke volume multiplied by heart rate), as well as your muscle's ability to extract and metabolize oxygen for sustained periods of time. The better your cardio-respiratory system, the longer you can exercise without fatigue and exhaustion.

Ok, we know it's important, and I mean "Oh the humanity, oh, the humanity" important, but the question arises: how do you improve your cardio-respiratory endurance? I'll make the answer as simple as possible: exercise harder and longer than you normally do.

The four elements to be considered for cardio-respiratory training and any kind of physical conditioning program are frequency, intensity, time and type, universally known as F.I.T.T. in the fitness industry. All of these parameters need to be pushed to "above normal" in order to see improvements in cardio-respiratory fitness (note how I said "above normal" and not "the limit of physical and mental sufferance"). Training needs to be fun and tolerable or else you're not going to stick with it. Know when to back off and rest. Let's look at each switch a little closer:

Frequency: Regardless of whether the exercise is cardio-respiratory or resistance-based, you need to do it at least three times a week.

Intensity: Depending on how good your ticker is and when the last time you exercised with any regularity, you should start anywhere from 50 to 70% of your maximum heart rate. How do you find out your maximum heart rate? Subtract your age from 220. That's it. It's that simple.

Type: Choose the specific exercises you need to perform in order to get the results you desire. For cardiovascular activity, choose exercises like running, swimming, cycling and chasing bad people. Resistance training involves working against opposing forces and exercises usually include weight lifting.

Time: Cardiovascular exercise needs to be at least 20 minutes (continuously, nonstop), while the time variances for resistance training is a little trickier to define and more open for personal adaption. Contracting the muscle (called the concentric phase of the lift) of a single repetition should be anywhere from three to five seconds. Pause for a second at the top of the movement when the muscle was fully loaded. At the eccentric portion of the lift, you might take anywhere from three to 10 seconds, depending on the level of hypertrophy you want to achieve and the amount of stress you want to impose on the worked muscle. Again rep tempo can vary wildly, depending on desired effect, experience, knowledge and fitness level.

NAVY SEALS IN TRAINING:

Yearn for exciting adventures in exotic locales? Be a U.S. Navy SEAL! Training is rigorous and fun, with applicants required swimming 50 meters wearing boots and full battle uniform and 3 miles with a wet suit. There's more: SEAL hopefuls learn to hold their breath underwater in depths up to 15 ft for 60 seconds, amid the fantastical marine ecosystem which includes sharks, crabs and stinging jellyfish! Tryouts also require thrill-seekers to do 90 push ups, 15 pull ups, 100 sit ups, and 60 dips and run a 7 minute mile in sand wearing boots. And then there's the beatings... but some things should be witnessed first hand!

CARVING UP ON CARDIOVASCULAR

There two ways to run: the right way and the wrong way. The right way will improve your cardio-respiratory endurance and carve up your body into a lean, aerodynamic machine. The other way is an exercise in futility.

What is the right way? Run at least 20 minutes at 60- 80% of your maximum heart rate. After 20 minutes your body will begin to tap into those cursed fat stores around the gut and elsewhere in a complex process called the Krebs cycle, along with the glucose floating in your blood stream (and to dispel any confusion, "blood sugar" and glucose are the same and are derived from carbohydrates). Thirty minutes and over and your body starts reaching for energy-rich fatty acids as its fuel and sparing the remaining glucose for the brain. This conversion from the metabolism of glucose (called glycolysis) to the metabolism of free fatty acids (called lipolysis) is gradual, and it takes at least 20 minutes to enter into this energy system. Recall that while glucose is fast, easy energy, it can run out in a hurry because it's only four calories per gram, while a gram of fat yields significantly more energy at nine calories. MCTs, a special kind of fat, have eight calories per gram.

THE TRICK TO TRACK

The trick to incinerating fat in the least amount of time is by doing cardiovascular activities that employ the whole body and spread out the workload to all the muscles. Good examples of 'whole body exercises' are cross country skiing and swimming, and on the resistance side of things: squats and deadlifts. These exercises recruit many muscles simultaneously, so you burn more energy in less amount of time. Remember: intensity is the secret ingredient to effective exercise, and that means investing 100% of your focus on whatever the task. Visualize the muscles contracting and stretching, the fat melting from your midsection. Imagine the new you.

While on the subject of intensity, you should know high-intensity cardio is best for burning fat. For those unfamiliar with the term, here is the definition of "high-intensity cardio": run as fat as you can for an allotted period of time (usually two minutes), slow down to a slow jog for 30 seconds, then go full throttle again. Repeat for 20 minutes to a half hour. Some people call them wind sprints or interval training while others call it pure unadulterated hell. Whatever affectionate name you give it, the high-intensity cardiovascular regimen as described here is more efficient at burning fat and spares more muscle (since it burns less calories but sheds more fat). In addition high intensity cardio kept metabolism hot like a blast furnace for over 24 hours, while the moderate intensity did not raise metabolism for any appreciable amount of time.

Perhaps the most important tip regarding cardio and burning fat is regarding the best time to run for maximal fat burning effect: the absolute best time to burn fat with cardio is after you wake up from sleep. You will have an empty stomach; blood glucose levels will be low (meaning your body will have to tap into fat stores right away for energy) and you will be well-rested... hopefully. You will also likely be in a catabolic state, so I heartily recommend drinking a glass of water with 5-10mg glutamine and supplementing with vitamin c and ideally desiccated liver tablets for a hit of protein and amino acids. Now you're ready for your run!

FEAR THE RUNNING GEAR

You need good running shoes. Running can be brutal on the body, and improper footwear can hasten injury and harvest blisters. If your unsure as to what running shoe suits you, go to an athletic footwear store where the salesperson looks like a marathon guru who drinks wheat grass juice for breakfast. You'll likely pay more in the end but all your questions will get answered and the shoe will rock. However, good running shoes don't *have* to cost bazillion dollars. The perfect running shoe for you may also be the most inexpensive. Buy the shoe that fits your foot and your budget.

As for the uberstyle'n sweat-neutralizing sports gear storming the market, they are definitely effective at wicking away sweat. Maybe *too* effective, says an interesting article by Nick Shulz in a September 2005 Slate magazine posting. By drawing perspiration from the skin before it can cool the body (as sweat is designed to), it may actually be sabotaging the bodies own natural thermal regulation capabilities. Ergo you sweat even more, get even hotter and dehydrate even faster.

The bottom line is don't let anyone tell you what you do and don't need.

You Tube

Title: **Marathon Training Schedule with Running Apparel Advice**

Tags: marathon running training 10k 5k race

From: Justrunnersdotcom

PREVENT BLISTERS AND STITCHES

If you're going to start running, first and foremost, make sure you get decent running shoes. It doesn't mean spending a mint, but go to a reputable retailer that specializes in athletic footwear and ask some questions. Get shoes that fit properly and have no "play" in them (that's shoe salesman talk for snug fitting). If your foot shifts around inside the shoe when you step, the constant friction will cause blisters, unnecessary wear and tear in the interior of the shoe and ruin many a sock! Running with bad footwear can make your muscles and joints feel like they've been taken out in the back alley and beaten with a bag of oranges. Your feet, which bear the brunt of the workload, will quit and join the witness protection program!

Another tip to preventing blisters is to keep your feet as dry as possible. According to a study at the University of Missouri-Columbia of athletic socks, cotton socks are the worst for causing blisters for walkers and runners. Cotton fiber retains 3x more moisture than acrylic and is downright thirsty compared to other performance-optimized hybrid fabrics on the market that wick away sweat as fast as your pores can pump it out. A wet sock tends to stretch and lose its shape inside the running shoe and resultantly, the sock will wrinkle and bunch up whilst you run, causing friction which inevitably leads to big juicy blisters.

You can always just apply Vaseline or Bodyglide beforehand to any areas of the foot which seem prone to blistering.

ALREADY GOT A BLISTER? If a big juicy blister has already formed on your foot mid-run, do what ultra marathoner Dean Karnazes does. He pops the blister and applies Krazy Glue to the affected area, which immediately binds and coats the skin super snug.

STITCHES ARE ANYTHING BUT. Ok, so now you're in full flight. You're feeling great and taking long powerful strides... and you suddenly feel as if a ninja has snuck from behind and plunged a knife is into your side! The sudden stabbing pain in the side is actually a cramp known as "stitches", and it is preventable. Here are a few ideas:

- The first thing you can try is to stretch beforehand. A simple and effective stretch would be to raise one arm above your head and bend to the side. Hold a deep but comfortable stretch for 30 seconds to a minute and alternate by raising the other arm and bending to the other side.

- Analyze your breathing next time you go for a jog. If you exhale when your right foot lands on the ground, you are especially prone to stitches on the right side. Why? The Doctors Book of Home Remedies for Men explains that the exhalation and impact of your step places downward pressure on the liver (which is on the right) and triggers a painful response aka side stitches. The solution is to exhale when the left foot steps, and see if that doesn't keep the ninjas at bay.

- I've also learned from various sources salty foods (like pretzels) or a small pre-race meal rich in potassium and vitamin c may prevent side stitches and cramps, but keep eating to a half hour or longer before the run. During your run, breathe deep and evenly through your mouth and nose and stay hydrated.

RECOVER FASTER AFTER LONG RUNS

We've all seen marathon runners that collapse into a quivering heap of flesh after they cross the finish line, and we feel the same want to get off our feet immediately after a hard and hellish run. However, according to Fitness Theory Manual (*2nd edition*), this is the worst thing you can do! Sudden stopping after exercise can cause blood or venous pooling (the combination of retention of blood in the muscles and gravities pull) which temporarily deprives the heart and brain of oxygen, and can result in fainting. It will also prolong your recovery time in the long term. So here's the hack: after a long run, don't stop. Keep moving. Keeps blood circulating in your muscles. You'll minimize muscle soreness and prevent the onset of nausea and fainting (and prevent you from looking like a big wuss bag).

RESISTANCE TO RUNNING

For approximately 30 minutes after resistance training, worked muscles are hungry and hyper-responsive to an insulin surge of nutrients and glucose. Supplementing with a post-workout drink (as described in this book) during this small window of opportunity is proven to be highly anabolic and build muscle faster. Beyond that 30 minute anabolic window, the benefits decrease dramatically.

So doing cardiovascular exercise for any time longer than 30 minutes directly after weightlifting would seem to compromise muscle acquisitions, making it an (ahem) exercise in futility. Slamming your post-workout shake afterwards and then doing a cardio workout is no good either, because now your insulin levels are elevated and fat burning is inhibited (not to mention the uncomfortable sloshing around in your stomach as you huff it on the treadmill).

The way around this conundrum (sort of) was by swallowing vitamin C and several desiccated liver tablets with glutamine water between resistance and cardio. This way starving muscles are tossed a few amino acids and catabolism is staved off for the time being.

You could also do cardio first or keep cardio activity after weight-training to 30 minutes maximum. Then consume your post-workout beverage immediately, before showering or anything else.

NINE FORMULAS OF FAST

The formula for fast is not all that complicated or secret. There are no injections, radioactive treatments or gene splicing with cheetahs. You won't need to run on a treadmill, wearing a respirator while scientists in lab coats copiously jot notes on clipboards. The steps are really quite simple, and are applicable to anyone achieving any goal in life. They are:

1) Set realistic but challenging goals. In this case, it'd be to run a predetermined distance at a faster pace than before. If your morning jaunt around the neighbourhood normally takes an hour to complete, determine to finish your run in 55 minutes.

2) Training systems including speed bursts, wind sprints and fartleks can increase foot speed, and uphill running is great for improving ballistic strength and speed, while building and strengthening the quadriceps with squats and leg presses will remove one more excuse to stop running before it is time. To improve your V02 max (how efficiently your body utilizes oxygen) there are two ways as described in a January 2007 issue of Wired. First is to conduct cardiovascular training with a mouth full of water. By limiting the volume of air to the lungs, you can force breathing muscles to be more resourceful and extending your peak performance. The second suggestion is high altitude training, or training in high heat which can supe endurance and even blood circulation.

3) Progressively increase perceived exertion and intensity so that your body must adapt to these greater demands, ergo becoming fitter over time. There are two easy ways of determining intensity and effort based on how vigorously you feel you are working, known as the Rating of Perceived Exertion (RPE). First is the original Borg scale developed by Swedish psychologist Gunnar Borg in 1982, and it ranges from 6 to 20.

4) Still, all the speed work in the world isn't going to help if you run like a pre-schooler with droopy drawers. Your running form needs to be tight and economized. Keep arms close to your side and hands open and pointing ahead to minimize air resistance (it makes a slight difference) and keep the chin up so you can breathe easy. Most of all, push off the balls of your feet like you want it bad!

5) Instead of pounding the pavement, step lightly. It's easier on the joints and ligaments and it will improve your agility and foot speed big-time.

6) To improve your acceleration from standing to full sprint, use small quick steps rather than long strides. See if you don't run like Flash Gordon with his red underwear on fire.

7) If you're *really* serious about being a faster runner, lose body weight. The less mass to lug around, the better one's VO2 Max (a measure of how well the body utilizes oxygen and a key physiological determinant of an athlete's speed and endurance). Energy expenditure will be lower getting from points A to B and your cardiovascular system will be taxed less, thus improving your VO2 Max.

8) Measure performance and report the results to others. Finally, when we reach our front door gasping and wheezing, we check our stop watch and measure our performance. If we fell short of our goal and only shaved a measly minute off the normal time, return to step one and devise a more realistic goal. Or look into gene therapy. If we meet or beat the 55 minute mark, rejoice and set a

new goal. Regardless of the results, share the news with others, be it friends, fellow runners or members of a runners online discussion forum. Repeat this three step program and with time and due diligence you'll be a winner at whatever you do.

9)   It's running during the night time, when pollution levels are lower and the adrenaline is pumping a little harder that we tend to run faster and can dig a little deeper. Familiar routes become more foreign in the darkness, which adds to the experience and our perceived rate of exertion is less, allowing us to do more.

RATING OF PERCEIVED EXERTION (RPE) SCALE

6 TO 11 = Very light exertion. A warm-up or cool down would be within these parameters.

12 TO 14 = A steady pace (approximately 60% Maximum Heart Rate) and just on the outskirts of the sissy zone.

15 TO 20 = A self rating of 15 is considered hard while 19 is really given'r (approximate MHR = 90%). 20 is projectile vomiting.

You can multiply your Rating of Perceived Exertion (RPE) by 10 and this should give you a reasonably accurate estimate of your actual heart rate during exercise. For example, if you deem you're giving it an honest 15, then 15 x 10 = 150, therefore your heart rate is approximately 150 beats per minute

---

The <u>Revised Rating of Perceived Exertion Scale</u> is probably easier to remember and work with, since it's on a scale from 0 to 10. It's on the next page.

Title: **Perfect running technique**

Tags: running technique tips jogging run jog sport exercise fitness

From: realbuzzvideos

RPE SCALE REVISED

0 = Either watching television or dead with eyes open.

1 = At this minimal level of exertion, you could carry on a lively conversation with yourself without catching your breath.

3 = "Ain't no thing but a chicken wing"

5 = Stepping' on the gas. This is when sweat starts to bead on your forehead, but it's a comfortable pace.

7 = Very strong effort

10 = Set cardio machine to kill!

A rating of 3 to 5 is typically the "fat burning zone". High intensity is an effort of 8 and above

As for increasing your workout intensity, do so gradually for a sustained period of time so your body can acclimatize itself to the faster pace.

HOWTO: MONITOR YOUR HEART RATE

Ok, you got your butt out of bed and ran around the block a few times. Good for you. Now you want to quickly monitor your heart rate and here's are two easy ways to accomplish this.

RADIAL ARTERY METHOD

Press your second and third finger on the radial artery. It's the groove on your wrist, directly below the thumb. Adjust the fingers so you can feel a slight pulsation, which is the blood moving into your hand. This is your heart rate... how often the heart is pumping out blood to the limbs, muscles and organs. Take your heart rate for 10 seconds, starting your count at zero and not one. Multiply your pulse count by six to get a count for one minute. Note that after 10 seconds your heart rate will slow and your reading will be inaccurate, so "timing" is everything.

CAROTOID ARTERY METHOD

Use two fingers (and not the thumb, as it has a pulse of its own) and apply slight pressure on the carotid artery, which is found alongside your trachea (windpipe). There are actually two carotid arteries which supply blood to the brain, so we only want to press slightly on one to get our count. Take your heart rate for 10 seconds, starting your count at zero and not one. Multiply your pulse count by six to get a count for one minute and again, take note that after 10 seconds your heart rate will significantly decrease and your reading will be inaccurate.

CALCULATE TARGET HEART RATE

The target heart rate is 65- 85% of your maximum heart rate, and is considered "the zone" for burning fat and accruing the benefits of cardiovascular activity. The Karvonen Formula is a mathematical recipe used to calculate where the zone is for you, but first you have to know your Resting Heart Rate, Maximum Heart Rate and Heart Rate Reserve:

1. RESTING HEART RATE (RHR) is a person's heart rate

at rest, and the best time to get this reading (either via radial or carotid artery) is in the morning, even before you stumble out of bed. In a normal person, the heart beats 60 to 80 times a minute, but it rises with age and the unexercised.

2. MAXIMUM HEART RATE (MHR) is your heart rate at maximum exertion, but the easiest way to determine this is simply 220 minus your age.

[The Karvonen formula for determining maximum heart rate (220-age) is not an exact science, but rather an estimate. It's accurate for ¾ of the population with a 10-15 bpm margin of error. There is also an alternative formula put forth by Londeree and Moeschberger from the University of Missouri-Columbia which is 206.3 – (0.711 x age).]

3. HEART RATE RESERVE (HRR) is the *difference* between maximum heart rate (MHR) and resting heart rate (RHR) and can be calculated by subtracting the (RHR) from the (MHR):
MHR – RHR = HRR. Once you know your heart rate reserve (HRR), you can determine where "the zone" is for you.

4. Here's where it gets a tad tricky. Multiply Heart rate Reserve (HRR) with your desired work intensity (65-85%) and add Resting Heart Rate (RHR) to determine your target heart rate/training zone. 85% work intensity is the high end of your training heart rate, 60% would represent the low end. Make note of the decimal:
(HRR X .85) + RHR = HIGH END; (HRR X .60) + RHR = LOW END

5. Now you know the range of how many beats per

minutes (bpm) you need to burn optimal fat (you can find out by taking your pulse for six seconds during

cardiovascular exercise and multiplying by 10). Stay within the high and low heart rate range for 30 to 60 minutes to burn maximum chunk.

Title: **Target Heart Rate**

Tags: Exercise TV star trainers

From: ExerciseTV

"ARE YOU THE UNDEAD?" TEST TO FIND OUT!

Capillaries are the smallest of the body's blood vessels, but they have the important responsibility of swapping oxygen and carbon dioxide between the heart and tissue cells. In living people that is. In the undead, the body doesn't have the ability to supply blood to the extremities (known as perfusion) because the heart is stone cold dead. That's why a zombie's skin get's green and clammy and limbs rot and fall off. You can make sure that's not you with this simple test.

1. Place your thumb on the person's fingernail and apply modest pressure.

2. The applied pressure will force blood away from the capillaries. Release pressure.

3. The fingernail should return to it's normal pink color within two seconds.

If color does not return promptly to the fingernail, there could be a number of factors at play, including a cold outside or room temperature, medications, or you're a dead corpse that has been brought back to life by a supernatural force. Visit a doctor for professional advice.

ENERGY CRISIS

THE CRISIS

Man continues his mindless obsession with life-depleting, non-renewable energy sources, and mortality is threatened to the brink of enfeeblement and obesity.

THE PLAN

Uncover arcanum secrets and ageless truths of carbohydrate consumption, achieving optimal energy and untapping the fountain of youth known as Human Growth Hormone (hGH). Unharness your superhuman energy levels and light up a world that grows ever so dark!

THE DEPARTMENT OF ENERGY

Did you know the human body has three separate mechanisms for creating energy, depending on the intensity and duration of the activity? I call them 'Immediate Response', 'Fight' and 'Flight', and they could save your life!

We'll start with something you should all be familiar with - the raw materials with energy: carbohydrates a.k.a. glycogen and fat, referred to as fatty acids, derived from the food we eat. Glucose and fatty acids are reprocessed into a highly specialized energy biochemical called Adenosine Tri-Phosphate (ATP) during the demands of aerobic and anaerobic exercise. Aerobic exercise is activity which utilizes lots of oxygen, and running, cycling and swimming all fall squarely into this category. Anaerobic exercise is just the opposite. It's a state whereby oxygen isn't used, typically because of the demands placed on the muscle.

The exercise is usually sudden and intense, and the body simply doesn't have the extra oxygen floating around - so the body does without - but for only up to three minutes.

We going to go back to ATP for a second, because it's impossible to underscore the importance of it's role in our lives. ATP is the currency of energy. You can't even scratch your butt without ATP, it's that important! What depletes ATP is intense cardiovascular exercise and resistance training, and it can take three, sometimes four days to replenish these muscle energy levels. Supplementing with creatine can help increase the amount of ATP in the body, since it's actually small pools of creatine phosphate (circa 3 oz distributed about the body) that combines forces with Adenosine Di-Phosphate (Di being the Greek root for "two") into Adenosine Tri-Phosphate. There's another jim-dandy supplement you can buy which synergizes well with creatine and is an actual component of ATP. It's called D-Ribose (ribose on the store shelves) and I can tell you from personal experience it's black gold for it's ability to reach that deep down power and energy to squeeze out one more rep or an extra 10 seconds of hard sprinting that you normally couldn't do. It's expensive as black gold too, so it makes sense only if you're serious about your training or want to smash a plateau that's keeping you down.

You Tube

Title: **ATP cycle**

Tags: ATP ADP cellular energy molecules phosphorylation dephosphorylation

From: SamuelHammer

Here are the three energy systems, IMMEDIATE RESPONSE, FIGHT and FLIGHT your body uses, in order.

ENERGY SYSTEM ONE: IMMEDIATE RESPONSE

Activity: Launching into a full sprint, ripping off the door of a burning car to save a trapped child

Time frame: The first 10 seconds - that's it. Then, provided there is a ready supply of Creatine Phosphate within the muscles, more ATP can be manufactured during a time of inactivity.

Energy system being engaged: ATP/Creatine phosphate

ENERGY SYSTEM TWO: FIGHT

Activity: Fighting for honour, truth and justice

Time frame: Up to three minutes

Energy system being engaged: Anaerobic Glycolysis (no O2) which produces lactic acid and the burn you feel in the muscles.

ENERGY SYSTEM THREE: FLIGHT

Activity: Running for your life, any type of heroic aerobic endeavor.

Time frame: Three minutes to indefinite.

Energy system being engaged: Lipid/fat utilization and aerobic glycolysis (w/ O2) in a process called the Krebs cycle.

MORE ABOUT WATER

Drink a lot of water throughout the day. It's energizing, metabolizing and flushes out toxins and fats. Tip: *Drinking ice cold water can help you lose weight, because the body expends roughly 17.5 calories warming and processing a 16-ounce glass ice water.*

A calorie is in fact called a kilocalorie, a kilocalorie is the amount of heat required to raise 1 kilogram of water by 1°C.

Think about it: under normal conditions, the human body dispels three quarts of water a day, more so if you workout, an alarming fact considering most people exist in a mild state of dehydration. According to the book The Healing Energies of Water by Charlie Ryrie, a mere two percent drop in hydration can slash energy levels by 20 percent. Dry mouth, headache, sunken eyes, dark yellow urine with a strong smell; these are symptoms of dehydration, and it can sneak up on anyone, even adults that know better. Children in particular need to be monitored vigilantly for these signs, because heck, they're busy being kids (and might not have access to water like we assume they might).

Suspect someone might be dehydrated? Here's a 10 second test you can perform to see if your right.

Pinch the skin on the back of the hand of an adult or the abdomen of a child, and hold for several seconds. Once released, the skin should snap back to it's former state. If it doesn't, or the delay in skin turgor is more than two seconds, we have a late symptom of dehydration. Here's what to do about it:

In 1 quart/liter of water, mix together these ingredients:

Table Salt - 3/4 teaspoon

Baking Powder - 1 teaspoon

Sugar -4 tablespoons

Orange juice - 1 cup

This is a formulation devised by the World Health Organization (WHO) to optimise adsorption of fluids into the body and should be ingested with frequent sips.

A good indication of your hydration level is your urine. If it's dark yellow and has a strong smell, you need to drink more water and, on the flipside, if you're peeing frequently and it's transparent with no noticeable odor, you can chill a bit. Drinking too much water can have a dangerous effect on your body's electrolyte balance (although this seems to be a rare problem in this society governed by caffeinated soft drinks and other diuretic beverages).

Finally, in regards to distilled vs. tap water, distilled water is quote/unquote better, but it's an unregulated industry meaning there are no defined and enforced standards of quality to adhere to. Your best bet is to opt for water which states "Natural Spring water bottled directly from the source" right on the label. Anything else could be tap water, not that tap water will *kill* you... yet.

[Approximately 65% of a males body composition is water, while with females it ranges anywhere from 43% to 63%. Muscle mass contains more water than fat, anywhere from 66-76% water to body fat's 20-30%. There's more. While your blood consists of 65-75% water, the brain and kidneys are over 80%!]

FOUR ENERGY UNLOCKING DEVICES

Camera gun... robot dog... cell phone with injectable vital-sign monitors... all of these James Bond gadgets might be cool to own, but they can't fire up energy levels instantly like these everyday energy unlocking devices you likely have on hand at the moment:

1. THE HUMBLE HOUSE PLANT

That's right. According to a study at Washington State University, having a house plant nearby can increase attentiveness and detoxify indoor areas where a wide array of cleaning products and electrical machinery give off volatile organic compounds (VOC) that can leach energy.

2. PEPPERMINT

Journal of Sport and Exercise Psychology reported a US study in 2001 that linked smelling peppermint with improved speed, strength and stamina. Whether it be the psychological lift of a comforting smell, or the clearing of the airways that peppermint provides hasn't been determined yet, but it seems to work!

3. THE SHOWER

We all feel invigorated after a shower, and often we attribute it to the private time we had to clear our mind and the water pounding on our back, but the cred belongs to electrically charged atoms called negative ions. Negative ions, dubbed "vitamins of the air" by Dr. Jim Karnstedt and Don Strachan, are created when are molecules are broken apart by shifting air and water and generate a positive biochemical response in our body and increase oxygen flow to the brain.

You Tube

Title: **EOS Anion Generator**

Tags: ANION Ionizer free radicals negative ions cluster

From: chiamtj

4. AN MP3 PLAYER

…or a disc player, or any contraption that can crank music loud and proud. There's a growing chorus of scientific and empirical evidence that proves loud music can instantly charge energy levels and relieve stress.

CARBS FOR ENERGY

If your energy levels are bottomed out and you feel stripped of strength, it's likely your body could use a high carbohydrate meal. Ideally, you want to opt for fibrous and nutritionally-dense complex and refined carbs, but go ahead and splurge on simple carbs (pastries, cereals, cake) to rebalance your energy deficit. Just don't overdue it (simple carbs are associated with many health problems, from raising the risk of cardiovascular disease to fatigue, skin eruptions, headaches and depression). If you're going to take in sugar, ingest a multivitamin as well because simple carbs deplete certain vitamins in the body and the uptake and adsorption of the vitamins and minerals is higher when insulin levels are higher.

When energy levels are decent, and your appetite is large and in charge, it's an idea opportunity to eat cheese, fish, eggs and other foods abundant in good fats and low in carbohydrates. Now would not be a good time for simple carbohydrates because they wouldn't provide lasting satiety, and you're likely to over-indulge. So here's the hack: eat high carbs when low on energy, and low carb when high on energy!

Here is a listing of the three types of carbs, complex carbohydrates being healthiest:

SIMPLE CARBOHYDRATES

Doughnuts, cake, soda pop, brown and white sugar, sweet fruit, fruit juice, candy, maple and corn syrup, honey, glucose, fructose, dextrose

REFINED CARBOHYDRATES

Unsweetened cereal, non-whole wheat breads, pasta, granola.

COMPLEX CARBOHYDRATES

Vegetables, legumes (peas, beans, lentils), nuts and seeds, whole grain bread, whole grain pasta, whole grain cereals

GUT FEELINGS - EXPLAINED!

We've all felt it, that gut feeling. That feeling of fear, love or stress that resonates not only in our mind but our body. Where is it from? How is it that we can feel emotion in our gut?

It's the lower intestine actually, all 22 mondo-important nutrient absorbing feet of it. The lower intestines is also comprised of a dense nerve infrastructure which carries 95% of the brains mood-regulating hormone called serotonin. Ninety-fricken-five percent! When you experience an emotion, you can be assured the neurotransmitter serotonin is the chemical messenger that carries the signal. Evidently, a lack of serotonin in the small intestines can cause irritability (known as irritable bowel syndrome) just as a lack of serotonin in the brain can cause irritability and depression!

Ok, I'm a believer you say. How can I improve the health of my brain and gut you ask. Eat yogurt and prunes I answer, as I place my hand on your shoulder and squeeze lightly. And fatty fish high in Omega 3, like sardines, herring and mackarel I add, smiling warmly. And read "More Microbe Than Human" I conclude.

MORE MICROBE THAN HUMAN

Next time you go on a gut feeling, make sure it's not the 10 trillion microbes (500-1000 species give or take) swarming in your stomach at any given time. In fact, there are more microbial cells in the human body than body cells! Gut microflora (aka bacteria) plays a crucial role in digestion and how much energy and nutrients we derive from our food. Symbiotic or "good" bacteria can make food go farther. Meanwhile, "pathogenic bacteria of evil" prevent the calories of ingested food from being properly utilized and leaks toxicants into the gastrointestinal system, harming the stomach lining. Bottom line: having the wrong mix of gut microflora can predispose you to obesity and low energy levels. Alternately, promoting the right microflora through proper diet and supplementation can help you look svelte and feel svell.

Symbiotic bacteria can be promoted by eating a diet high in prebiotics and probiotics. Prebiotics are non-living dietary supplements, for instance soluble and insoluble fibre and fructo-oligosaccharide which is found in a variety of fruit and vegetables. Probiotics, on the other hand, contain live bacteria and can be found in yogurt and supplements like bifidoacteria and lactobacilli. And according to recent research findings, high fat diets (like Keto-Fu which promote ketosis) can positively change the gut's microbial metabolic signature (whether it's because of microbial or gene activity is still unknown).

Flex magazine recommends eating 10-15 grams of total fibre per 1000 calories (no more than 5 grams at a time) and a small portion of yogurt several times a day, especially with meat.

CIRCADIAN RHYTHM RADIO

With all due respect to Greenwich Village Time, work buzzers, agendas and time clocks - they really have little influence on how our bodies keep time.

The secret, omnipresent timekeeper governing how we feel and when, is a physiological process called circadian rhythms, and it's on this watch we need to map out our activities.

Circadian rhythms, and there are over 100 of them, lay the grooves for 24 hour sets and regulate every function of our bodies. Heart rate, body temperature, energy levels, quantity and quality of sleep, pain tolerance and so forth, are conducted by these overlapping and on going rhythms like a rave party.

The disc jockeys mixing these phat basslines is found in a miniscule section of the brain called the suprachiasmatic nuclei. It receives and processes internal and external clues such as light, dark, food and energy, and keeps body functions synchronised with these events in a synergistic manner. When we're synced with our environmental stimuli, we feel alive and ready for action. When our rhythms skip a beat, the repercussions can be profound and long-lasting. We can't sleep properly, our energy levels suck and we feel vulnerable.

24 HOUR CIRCADIAN CYCLES

Here's the typical circadian playlist and how you can keep it locked all day long.

5AM - DJ Fahrenheit drops the body temperature to its lowest point of the night, and as a result we sleep better.

6AM - As your body temperature starts to rise, you awake and start your day proper. Rhythms that govern sleep stop

and other rhythms, triggered by outside influences called "zeitgebers", initiate other cycles. Light and darkness are big ones. Blood pressure also rises in the morning (and maybe even your temper when you realise it's only Tuesday). Also: Drivers are 20 times more likely to nod off at the steering wheel at this time, so avoid driving if at all possible.

8AM - Coritisol levels are highest in the mornings and this is not necessarily a good thing. Cortisol is a hormone produced by the adrenal cortex as a response to stress and increases blood pressure. Cortisol also wastes muscle tissue, so if you're keen on keeping your hard-earned muscle, 8am is a good time to reverse it's affect by downing a protein shake.

10AM - Heart attacks are three times more likely around this hour than any other time of the day. This may be due to a) caffeine and other stimulants people use to wake and get the motor running, b) the relatively sudden physical and mental activities from the dormant, ultra-relaxed state of sleep, and c) increases of cortisol in the blood.

12PM - Lunch is another zeitgeber that gives the brain hints as to whether active circadian rhythms are on the beat. Noon is typically when we are in the best mood of the day (provided you avoided the 10 am heat attack). Go hither and make friends and influence people.

1PM - Medical studies suggest meds are best administered at this time. Something about the afternoon makes the potency and effectiveness just that much better.

2PM - Hand/eye coordination peaks at 2 pm, giving you the manual dexterity to pwn villains and videogames and surpass production standards at work.

4PM - Pain tolerance is highest at 4pm, so schedule your next dentist appointment at this time. You can also squeeze out a few more reps at this golden hour.

5PM - When's the best time for no-holds barred cage match you ask? Why, it's at 5pm, when your muscles are strongest and most pliable!

6PM - If supper-time makes you sing, it's because tastebuds are at their keenest at the dinner hour.

8PM - Let's face it, abstaining from alcohol is best, but if you do drink, remember that alcohol tolerance is highest at this hour, and it would be easy to hurt yourself by consuming too much. Drink responsibly, if you must at all.

11PM - Sleep triggers a release of growth hormone and all the action happens within the first two hours. Capitalise on this important opportunity for recuperation with a ZMA stack and 5mg of glutamine dissolved in water.

3AM - Question for the women: Did you put on a skin moisturizer to capitalise on the skin-cell repairing that happens at this hour? You can avoid nasty pillow wrinkles by applying sunblock to your face before you go to bed.

ALL-NATURAL hGH SUPER STIMULATORS

You can wring every last drop of advantage and benefit from exercise by eating foods that will elicit a better than average growth hormone response. Just remember to eat at least a half hour before your workout to avoid feeling bloated and gassy.

SUPER HUMAN BEANS

Next time you see fava and velvet beans in the local super(hero)market, toss them in the grocery cart. Both kinds of beans contain about 15% L-Dopa (l-dihydroxyphenylalanine), which in turn converts to the neurotransmitter dopamine, the chemical in the brain largely responsible for the jacked-up feeling you get after a heavy lift. Fava and velvet beans also increase growth hormone.

B6 = hGH

B6 supplementation aids the body in the utilization of amino acids and muscle glycogen and can trigger a significant hGH response with strenuous activity. As with everything else, consult your doctor to determine a dosage right for you.

MAXIMIZE YOUR hGH RESPONSE

Somatostatin is the body's chemical signal to stop growth hormone release, which is why you don't see Somatostatin invited to too many parties. What suppresses Somatostatin is L-Arginine, the amino acid extraordinaire and Alpha Glyceryl-phosphorylcholine ("alpha say wha?"), a metabolite derived from soya lecithin. Both can be found as supplements at your local health food store.

NEGATIVE CALORIES, NEGATIVE ENERGY?

Heard the urban legend of how some vegetables are so low in calories you actually burn more calories to eat and digest them than they offer? Theoretically, if you ate enough of said vegetables over time you would eventually starve to death! But is it true?

Vegetables such as celery, Chinese cabbage, cucumber and lettuce actually *do* require more energy to chew and digest than they supply, and if you ate enough for long enough, I suppose you would indeed shuffle off this ole mortal coil.

Let's punch in the numbers: a 190lb individual burns up 114 calories just sitting on his butt reading this section, then another 228 calories ill-advisedly preparing the Pe-Tsai cabbage to eat. Already he or she is 34 cups of Chinese cabbage in the hole. Yes, being that one cup of Chinese cabbage offers a mere 10 calories, they'd need to eat a smidgen over 34 cups to ever meet the caloric cost of those two activities. Then there's the caloric cost of eating the cabbage too, and you can see how a large caloric deficit can be created from eating these vegetables.

KEEP THE BODY GUESSING

Ever wonder why some souls, although they toil in the gym day after day and year upon year, never seem to change in how they look? It's due to the fact they do the same exercises, using the same weights and their own bodies have long since adapted. Such is the reason one needs to mix up exercises and keep things fresh. It keeps the body guessing, growing and responding the way you want it to. Strive to know 10 exercises per body-part, and rotate them regularly.

The same goes for cardiovascular exercise. Ever hear how long-time dedicated distance runners can no longer seem to shed fat, no matter how much they pound the pavement? The reason is their bodies have adapted to the rigors of running. It's analogous to a factory which streamlines its processes and minimizes its costs in producing a product.

The solution is to switch it up. Do several different cardio exercises (of the same intensity) in a session rather than just one exercise and it'll burn more energy (which in most cases means more body fat). For example, doing the stair climber machine alone for an hour is good, but 20 minutes stair-climber, proceeded immediately with 20 minutes running, preceded immediately with 20 minutes cycling will burn more energy. An even better solution is to incorporate resistance training into your routine and cut way back on the cardio. The human body, unlike our stuffy old selves, love change. Remember, a good rule of thumb is, if you go a particular exercise more than three times in a row, it's time to put it on the shelf for awhile and try something new.

WE'VE MET BEFORE: DETERMINING CALORIC EXPENDITURES

Think of a MET (a sort of acronym for Metabolic Equivalent) as a unit. A single MET is how much oxygen your body cashes in at rest, and the number goes up proportional to the intensity of the activity engaged in. Simply put, one MET is equal to 3.5 ml of oxygen per kilogram (kg) of body weight per minute (multiply your weight in lbs by 2.2 to convert into kg).

The *caloric expenditure* of one MET is equal to your own unique Basal Metabolic Rate (BMR). You may recall the formula for determining your BMR I showed you elsewhere in the book, and I'll repeat it here:

BMR=BODYWEIGHT(LBS) X (11 FOR MALE, 10 FOR FEMALE) / 24

which simply means multiply your weight (in lbs) by either 11 or 10 and divide the number by 24 hours. Figure that out and you know how many calories it takes to maintain you at a resting state. have the value of a MET for you.

Gravy so far. To find out how many calories you're burning during any particular activity, just consult the MET chart and multiply your BMR/MET (you say chicken, I say fish) by that number. For example, light housework has a "rating" of two METS, so if you're a 200 lb male, a MET for you is 91.6 calories per hour multiplied by two. Ergo light housework will burn 183 calories for this individual. Swimming in lime green Jell-O ™ is a whopping 12 METS (91.6 x 12). An hour of such silliness would cost 1099 calories (provided you don't drown or eat it all) which makes me think we should all start doing it.

Here is a list of activities and their MET values for your perusal:

2 METS/HR: light housework, walking at a slow pace, animated conversation, echolocation

2.5 TO 3 METS/HR: golfing (using power cart), fishing, walking at an average pace, slow dancing, reality warping

3.5 TO 4.5 METS/HR: golfing (with caddie), walking at a brisk pace, climbing stairs, falling down stairs (lol), volleyball, table tennis, calisthenics, sweeping the floor

5 TO 6 METS/HR: golfing (carrying clubs), shoveling snow, slow leisurely jog, doubles tennis,"gettin' your groove on fo' da ladies", leisurely cycling, hiking, hunting, skating

7 TO 8 METS/HR: swimming, hockey, tennis (singles), racquetball, backpacking, handball, soccer, saving a small child from a burning building,basketball

9 TO 12 METS/HR: hard running, cross-country skiing, contact football, fencing, mortal combat with arch enemy, gymnastics

THE KETO-FU DIET

THE CRISIS

Fear. Uncertainty. Doubt. That's exactly what's being published by some vegetarians, rehearsed by brainwashed citizens and spouted by high-carb zealots about ketogenic diets.

THE DIET

You need to find out the truth and expose the lies for yourself and for the benefit of all mankind. Learn how ketones are not only an invaluable backup fuel source for the body and brain, but a healthy and sustainable physiological state.

KETOSIS KOMPLIANCE

There are a number of conditions you should comply with before making these incredible planet-smashing changes to your diet. In the Keto-Fu Diet, you will be severely restricting carbohydrates, and you won't be able to have fruits and vegetables any ole time you want. Being in the state of ketosis for the first time is like coming down with the flu. You need to be primed for this kind of radical physical transition. Please go through the list below and make sure you can put a big fat check mark beside each one before you start.

Go see a doctor and get a physical examination. Make sure you are well. If you're suffering depression or plagued with anxiety or stress, a low glycemic, low-carb diet emphasizing good fats can do wonders, as it has for me. But physically, it helps to be in good shape. You shouldn't be nursing an injury or even recovering from a hard workout, as carbohydrates are important in the speedy repair of muscle fibers. If you have a cold, experience chronic fatigue or insomnia or have any nagging infections, hold off until these health problems are resolved and stick with a balanced diet rich in fresh fruits and a variety of vegetables. Again, on a ketogenic diet such as the Keto-Fu, fruits and vegetables can only be eaten at specific times when the sugars can be quickly spent by the body so ketosis can be re-established.

If you are severely overweight, you should hold off on this diet until you are anywhere within 15-25% body fat. Anymore adipose may result in sagging, excess skin because of how rapidly you will lose weight. It's like calling the whole X-Men crew into action when Professor X could do it alone from his wheelchair! Instead, try a conservative weight loss strategy which integrates moderate exercise.

Get blood work done and find out your TG/HDL ratio. TG stands for triglycerides and HDL stands for the good cholesterol High Density Lipoprotein which you will learn about later. Also get your blood glucose levels checked to make sure Type 2 Diabetes isn't looming in your future. If you have not-so-stellar results from these tests, don't worry, The Keto-Fu Diet is perfectly suited to address these problems. You should know your blood type. If you don't, this is a good excuse to find out. Red meats and fats jibe better with some blood types (type O for example) than others (type A), so knowing what ketogenic-friendly foods will harmonize with your immune system and digestive tract will increase you're likelihood of success.

Be prepared. As stated earlier, eating fruits and vegetables are restricted to certain times of the day, but they're not forbidden. Quite the opposite, they are more important than ever and will help you not only keep your health,you're your sanity when the times get tough. Keep antioxidant and vitamin rich fruits like pineapples, mangos and blueberries at the ready for when you see a window of opportunity (i.e. right before a work) to eat them and burn them off ASAP. I also recommend frozen vegetable mixes like California of Sante Fe style which will optimize the variety and range of vegetable intake. Consult the upcoming Keto-Fu grocery list for further suggestions.

Are you disciplined? Being in a state of ketosis can be physically draining. You'll likely experience fatigue, headaches and occasional nausea on the first few attempts. Normal tasks will seem more taxing, and when your muscles are in a glycogen-depleted state, they will burn whenever employed. But "the burn" is a good sign, and is usually the trigger of a hormonal response ala HGH (human growth hormone). You may feel like giving up, but you need to have the determination and discipline to keep your eyes on the prize and away from the carbohydrates.

A final caveat: When the brain is cut off from glucose and must rely on ketones for its power supply, the lights may be dim for awhile if you catch my drift. Your computational powers may slow a tad, especially the first time you achieve ketosis. Your thinking may be cloudy. If you're forgetful at the best of times, in ketosis you may walk out the house and go to work without pants on. But not to fear, symptoms are rarely that severe, but you may be one of the unlucky few who have a really difficult time with the transition.

THE INS OF INSULIN

Even if you don't know a lick about regulating blood glucose levels or appreciates the importance of controlling insulin and glucagon, that's ok. This diet is a great way to learn. You begin to understand how the body responds to different types of foods. Some foods will coax the pancreas to secrete mass amounts of insulin. On this diet you will learn what foods trigger the secretion of this hormone, why insulin is such an awesome anabolic hormone and when you should harness its abilities - and when to keep it controlled. As we discussed earlier, insulin's counterpart is the hormone glucagon, they both tightly regulate blood glucose levels.

INSULIN IN ACTION

We'll start with that tomato on toasted seven grain bread sandwich you just ate. The body will break this down, starting with the saliva and on to the stomach, which is passed on to the small intestine where most of the digestion takes place. The food is reduced into nutrients, amino acids and "The Amazing Sugar Duo" fructose (a quickly absorbed sugar derived from fruit) and glucose (another sugar derived from pretty much anything *but* fruit. Fructose is a good guy but is quickly stored as fat if not claimed by the liver or immediate energy demands of the body. Glucose, on the other hand, is released into the blood stream and has better staying power.

The higher your blood sugar level is, the stronger the insulin response will be to try and reinstate balance in the body (known as homeostasis). Insulin's job is to do collect up the glucose and fructose and store it away into various cells of the body.

Sooo, carbohydrates = glucose = sugar, right? Right. Full stop. However, some foods convert to sugar easier than others, and this is often referred to as their glycemic value. Diabetics have been using the Glycemic Index for some time to determine the conversion rate of different foods into blood glucose, and you should become familiar with it too. The Glycemic Index rates foods from 0 -100, the higher the number, the higher the payload of glucose. Know the glycemic value of everything you eat. Brain fart: Eat with purpose and not just habitually.

GLUCAGON AND INSULIN

We've been talking up insulin like it's the only game in town, but it isn't. Glucagon - not to be confused with the amino acid cum supplements Glutamine - is no also-ran. It's an ally of insulin but has the opposite effect. While insulin hives away glucose into body cells when blood sugar levels are high (the liver is on the take too, storing up large amounts of glucose), glucagon *frees up* glucose from the liver into circulation when blood sugar levels are low. In simplest terms, glucagon is an energy-releasing hormone and the opposite of insulin. It takes Free Fatty Acids out of fat cells, thereby initiating the elaborate process of oxidation and ketogenesis in the liver. When this happens, your body goes into a metabolic condition known as ketosis...

GET TO KNOWSIS KETOSIS

First off, know that ketosis rocks. Being in a state of ketosis is the Holy Grail of weight loss. It's a prime metabolic state for positive hormonal activity in the body (increased testosterone levels, growth hormone response) as well as highly thermogenic. The Keto-Fu Diet is based on ketogenic principles which explain why it's so staggeringly effective.

When in a state of ketosis, stored body fat becomes the fuel du jour when it ketosis. In ketosis, you will burn fat, even with minimal exertion. Fat is also an inefficient fuel source - the body has to work harder to convert it to energy - a doubleplusgood for the dieter. Being in a state of ketosis allows a more frequent and more powerful growth hormone response. In low carb diets, in particular the ketogenic diet when you'll be in a state of ketosis a great deal of time, you'll be prone to more growth-hormone surges (which as you know is the very fountain of youth), as well as Insulin-like Growth Factor-1 (IGF-1) and testosterone for the boys, critical components to muscle building and preservation.

DESTINATION: KETO COUNTRY

The method by which we achieve said incredible fat burning action is by restricting carbohydrate intake to practically nothing, couple with moderate exercise. Fasting for 24 hours will do it too. When in Keto country, insulin – the bad boy of hormones – is off the streets. The absence of insulin allows other hormones like glucagon to arise and unlock imprisoned body fat to run wild in the blood stream.

"NO CARBS? WHERE DO I GET MY ENERGY?"

Stored body fat won't be enough to supply energy and restorative materials for an active person, never mind a crime fighting champion of justice. The body will (at the first chance it gets) glean energy and amino acids from your own muscles in what are called catabolism. Think of catabolism as cannibalism of yourself! To prevent this gross evil-doing and to maintain ketosis, our diet must consist of mainly good fats (circa 70%) for long lasting energy and, to a lesser degree, protein to provide amino acids and prevent catabolism.

For rookies in particular, there can be the chilling psychological effect of eating upwards of 70% total calories from fat, even if it's good fats. Overcome that social/nutritional taboo and you stand to lose a lot of body fat in a short period of time. Cheese, whole eggs, beef and pork are all acceptable foods. Apply oils, butter and salad dressing liberally over vegetables - it's all part of the master diet to lose weight safely. Over the week, you will lose weight and body fat.

Sure, some of the weight lost is water (carbohydrates tend to retain more fluids than protein – hence the name carbo<u>hydrates</u>), but you'll shed the weight so fast you'll step on the scale again just to make sure you're not imagining things. What other "diet" (I'm beginning to hate that word, but let's suffer with it) allows, yea verily even recommends us eat fatty meats like steak, pork chops, bacon and all manner of foods you once shunned?! Shock your friends as you liberally use "regular" salad dressings and mayonnaise and chomp on chunks of cheese as if it was celery stalk, and lose weight. Fat, ironically enough, can help you lose fat! Friends and co-worker will comment on your quick weight loss. That cute girl working at the cash register will shoot you a look. And you'll unfortunately feel like warmed over death. At least for the first time as your body, and in particular your brain, adjusts to using ketones and not glucose as its primary fuel source. Let's look at why ketosis is "all that and a side order of bacon". Everyday activities will burn more calories and more body fat in a state of ketosis than when in a "normal" state when the body is using carbohydrates. And who wants to be normal?

LOVE HANDLES ARE A BATTLEFIELD

You've probably realized those stubborn love handles are the first to appear and the very last to go. Getting rid of them on a normal diet may be an epic conflict that extends beyond the reaches of time! There is a hormone receptor we can blame for this, its called alpha-2 (A2) and they are naturally produced adrenoreceptors which predominate in lower body fat cells and make those frustrating flaps of flesh so hard to get rid of. Worse yet, traditional low calorie diets actually coax the adrenal glands at our two kidneys to produce more of these receptors, which only make the problem more pronounced! The Keto-Fu Diet can reverse this demoralizing trend. In a state of ketosis your body becomes very efficient at mobilizing midsection fat and using it for energy or ushering it out through the bladder. So, the money line is: ketosis removes midsection fat fast!

FAT OF THE LAND

If you're new to the Keto-Fu Diet, you'll find the first day difficult. It's a radical paradigm shift from what most people are taught to believe. If you find it psychologically unsettling to eat cheese and bacon when you're trying diligently to lose the gut - that's normal. You will need to eat upwards of 70-80% fat with zero carbs on the first few days to instigate ketosis, but it's not as insane as it sounds. You'll see how easy it is to achieve those ratios a little further down in the ketomath section. Keep in mind, it's not "excess" fat that you're consuming, it's all within a relatively normal daily caloric total. If on a usual "non-dieting" day you would consume 2250 calories, on your first day on The Keto-Fu Diet you would reduce your total daily calories 15% to roughly 1900 calories. Of that 1900 calories, 80% should ideally be fat, be it polyunsaturated, EFA's, a smattering of saturated fats - what have you. The rest, 380 calories, would be protein and only trace carbs that your body wouldn't even compute.

Here are some reasons why you need to ingest so much fat:

- To prevent a possible downward spiral of the metabolism. Cutting caloric consumption too dramatically will be counterproductive.

- Carbohydrates are insulin inducing and will sabotage your efforts to get into ketosis... and even protein has anti-ketogenic effects. More than half of the dietary protein you eat will convert to glucose which will encourage an insulin response, so even protein intake must be kept to modest portions during initial phase of The Keto-Fu Diet. Simply put: moderate to high insulin levels = bad.

- By ingesting so much fat, you're practically teaching (not shocking) the body to resort to fat as it's primary fuel source. Provided your activity level is high enough (and this diet is definitely not for sedentary folk) and the macro nutrient ratios are dialed in properly, your body will have no option but to convert to Free Fatty Acids. There will be nothing else.

Dieters should first know what their daily "maintenance" caloric consumption is (a good way to do this is record everything you eat for 3-5 days, then take an average), then adjust 10-15% lower and divide by the number of meals you'll eat (make it a minimum of six). This will be your daily caloric intake during the Keto-Fu Diet.

One thing I've noticed is how fat phobic people are. Most do not allow enough fat in their diets, which leads to dry skin, nails and hair, hormonal imbalances and even neurological distress. People should only stay away from trans fats, which do the body no favors. All other fats, including saturated fat, have its benefits. I've heard unbelievers wonder aloud if the body would go into distress eating more fat than usual, but this is not the case if it's good fats (you'll be briefed extensively on good and bad fats in the upcoming chapter "Stacking Up the Evidence"). If anything, people, me included, feel more relaxed and even Zen-like while in ketosis.

After ketosis is established, you can even the protein/fat ratio out a bit more: fat = 55% protein = 30% and carbohydrates = 15% provided the carbs are eaten before resistance training and not cardio. Why not before cardio? Here's why: carbohydrates convert to glucose in the body, thereby raising your insulin level. When insulin levels are elevated, fat burning cannot occur.

This allows me a smooth transition to another critical aspect of establishing ketosis: exercise. Cardio will serve you best in the morning on an empty stomach or any other time you're trying to expel your body of glucose and muscles of muscle glycogen. Cardio brings on ketosis quickest, so break out the New Balance and run for at least a half hour. Full body resistance training is alright during this time, as long as you go use a high-rep scheme (15-20+) with no rest between sets to add an aerobic component. Keep the weight to no more than 50% of your one rep max and never going to failure. When muscles are glycogen -depleted, the micro-tears in the muscle fiber take longer to recover, and you're not trying to build muscle here. You can supplements with a high glycemic post-workout drink afterwards, but if you're striving to get into ketosis ASAP, leave it at that. In order to transition quickly back into ketosis, make your post-workout meal (give or take an hour after your post-workout shake) primarily dark green veggies with protein (for example, meat and fresh spinach with olive oil). The post-workout bevy you had earlier will suffice for carb replenishment and muscle growth.

Title: **Exercise: It's Non-Negotiable**

Tags: Atkins Diet Weightloss Low Carb Exercise Obesity Fat

From: bowulf

[If you're not either trying to obtain or maintain ketosis, keep fat calories to no more than 30% of your diet. Studies have demonstrated 97% of all fat calories assimilated by the body is converted to body fat, which can contribute to heart, colon and breast cancer. The long and short is this: <u>don't ride the fence.</u> The Keto-Fu Diet requires commitment, execution and the *avoidance of carbohydrates*. Fats will become the body's fuel now and during the duration of the diet. Wafflers belong at the International House of Pancakes!]

<u>FOOD ALGEBRA</u>

We know carbohydrates are the bodies preferred (but not exclusive) fuel source. What you may not know is fat has more calories per gram (9) than protein (4) or carbs (4), so high-fat foods tend to be more calorie-intense with every bite.

Generally, any food not needed for energy will be converted to stored body fat (the exception being ketosis). Ketosis makes fat storage metabolically impossible because body fat is being utilized as fuel. When in a state of ketosis, excess protein and fat in the digestive system is converted into blood glucose in a process called gluconeogenesis and then distributed into various cells of the body via insulin, or passed through the urine. Taking liberal amounts of vitamin C would convert much of that fat to collagen, and amping up your metabolism with apple cider vinegar tablets, C.L.A. or an orange bitter extract/L-Carnitine concoction (found at most health food stores) will help keep traffic moving. In any case, moderation and portion control is vital, even when on a strict low carb diet.

But how do you know what foods combinations help what foods hinder? Here's a simple formula: eat carbohydrates and protein together, or fat and protein together, but never carbohydrates and fat in the same meal. Carbs+Protein, Fat + Protein but never Carbs + Fat. Green fibrous vegetables do not count as carbs, because they cannot be converted to energy like normal carbs.

BEFORE AND AFTERMATH

If that equation made you all warm and tingly, you'll be happy to hear there is more. I call it <u>ketomath</u>, and its simple formulas can help you get into ketosis without overdoing fat and caloric consumption. For the first day or so, I recommend bacon, sardines/herring/tuna and chicken (they're all devoid of carbs), and add good fats like flaxseed or olive oil. For example, I'll open up a can of tuna and drench it in olive oil. No fuss, no muss, and no flavor, so I'm never tempted to overeat. A can opener is a single guy's most used utility! If you want to measure everything, that's fine. The Keto-Fu Diet is great for math geeks (which I am not) who like to crunch numbers and Pepsi cans with psychokinetic powers.

I'm now going to throw some numbers at you. Ready? To induce a state of ketosis through diet, you need upwards of 70% of your caloric intake to be fat for at least 48 hours. Can you pull off ketosis with even a lower fat percentage.

 Say a fat ratio of 50%? The answer is yes, IF you're overall caloric consumption is low enough. You see, if you fast, you can reach ketosis no prob. However, you are starving yourself and your body will take its energy from your muscles. That's bad. We want to spare our hard-earned muscle by ingesting enough fat, which will in turn stave of catabolism. The Keto-Fu Diet is very anti-catabolic and muscle sparing, more so than any other conceived diet.

You can tweak macro-nutrient ratios as you establish ketosis midweek, but you need to go heavy on fat in the beginning. The can of tuna has 140 calories. 30 grams is protein, 1 gram is fat, no carbs. The extra virgin olive oil is 183 calories per 2 tbsp serving. It has no carbs, no protein, but 9.2 grams is fat, most of it harmless monosaturates. I never measure anything, I go on what looks right. With practice and experience, you will instinctively know portion sizes, when you're in ketosis, when you're not. Don't lose your mind. If you've eaten too much, you can always punish yourself in the gym.

You Tube

Title: **Net Carbs vs. Net Effective Carbs - Marketing Hype**

Tags: Atkins Diet Weightloss Low Carb Sugar Alcohols Fitness

From: bowulf

Back to our can of tuna and olive oil, I'll guesstimate 4 tablespoons will make our 70% fat quota. Let's punch it into the calculator:

183 / 2 = 91.5 calories per tbsp.

91.5 x 4 tbsp = 366 calories

183 + 366 = 549 for total calories.

Now we're going to find out what percentage of total caloric intake this can of tuna is:

140 / 549 x 100 = 25.5% (25.5% of our meal/snack is tuna).

The remaining 74.87% is fat. This meal isn't exactly glamorous, but it sports 30 grams of protein and enough fat the keep your body in a testosterone fueled, anti-catabolic state of alpha-maleness. Nothing wrong with carbs, but it'll never make you feel so good.

If you insist on being precise in what you eat, you need to know the other part of this formula. Not every gram is equal: a gram of carbohydrates and a gram of protein are 4 calories, but a single gram of fat is 9 calories. A can of boneless herring fillets has 17 grams of protein, 2 grams carbs and 8.3 grams of some quality fats like omega 3 and 6 and monounsaturates. We're going to eat one can and we want to determine whether it meets our 70% threshold. First, we'll combine the protein and carbohydrates and multiply by 4 to find out the total calories for the two:

---

17 + 2 = 19 x 4 = 76 calories

8.3 X 9 = 80.1 calories for the fat.

76 + 80.1 = 156.1 total calories for this can of herring fillets.

80.1 / 156.1 x 100 (multiplying by 100 moves the decimal space two over... now it's all coming back you say) = 51.3%

Ketosis can be difficult (in particular for first-timers) to achieve and equally difficult to stay there. Once ketosis is achieved, sure, re-adjust your macro nutrient ratios. The Keto-Fu Diet takes practice, and you will get better at it as you cycle on and off. If you do eat or drink something that kicks you out of ketosis, don't fret. You will likely re-establish it in a short period of time.

KETOGENIC TIMELINE: WHAT TO EXPECT AND WHEN

This should not be a scientific diet. Sure there are rules, math formulas and monitoring devices like ketostix, calipers, thermometers - you name it - but you don't need them. Learn to read your own body instead. That old truism "Practice makes perfect" certainly applies here. Experimentation, education, trial and error are the best ways to becoming an efficient fat burning machine and controlling the way you look and feel. I used ketostix for the first few cycles, because it was part of the learning process for me, but they are unreliable as are all things in this world. Rely on yourself. What you see in the mirror, the taste in your mouth, the feel of your body will give you the most reliable reading of how well you're progressing toward your goals.

FIRST 24 HOURS: In the first 24 hours or so, you may not feel much of anything. Many factors come into play here: whether you fasted beforehand, the quantity of fat ingested, your metabolic rate and the list goes on. An initial "acknowledgment" from your body that you've made a major dietary change is you may feel your skin tighten. You won't notice a visual change, but your flesh will feel taut against your muscles. For me it's in my chest area. Your mileage may vary. High fat diets also induce a surge in testosterone production with the high fat in your system, so

much so you'll be fighting the urge to rip a phone book apart (but don't, you'll need it to order chicken wings). As touted earlier, high-fat, moderate protein foods take longer for the body to digest, so a feeling of contentment will prevail longer than the low-fat carbohydrate meals that your stomach makes quick work of. When you feel satiated for longer stretches of time, it's easier to restrict calories.

FIRST 2 DAYS: As blood glucose levels slalom, the testosterone euphoria you enjoyed earlier will likely be replaced with lethargy. If you're used to eating fresh fruits and vegetables everyday, the adjustment will be particularly odious. You'll feel like your health is going to hell in a hand basket. If you're a shiny-faced, happy-go-lucky fruit-eating tree hugger who can't go a day without an injection of citrusy, vitamin-loaded enzymes, take heart. You can still sneak them in, but ketosis will be broken and must be re-established either with cardio or waiting until liver glycogen depletes (which all depends on how much fruit you ate). Dark green fibrous vegetables are a little different. It's preferable to be firmly constituted in ketosis before introducing spinach, broccoli , kale to your meals (using olive oil or butter liberally to maintain ratios natch), but it's not nearly as disruptive as fruit. Just be sure to select low GI foods that are loaded with vitamins and other healthful properties.

You'll find the first 48 hours are a test of fortitude. Be strict with the high-fat phase and get into ketosis ASAP, and you'll reduce cholesterol levels and utilize fat, including body fat. Visualize yourself with a carved-up six pack and skin that looks thin and tight on your muscles (if that's what yanks your crank). Keep your focus.

You may notice flu-like symptoms including elevated body temperature, foggy mind, slowed reaction time and -for an unlucky few - mild nausea. I sometimes know (or think I know) the exact moment I've reached ketosis, because my

brain will suddenly get headachy, a sure sign it's converted from glucose to ketones. Normally I hate headaches and

run for the medicine cabinet (migraines have learned me good) but these headaches are mild and their sojourn is short-lived. They last half a day and dissipate as my brain

---

113

customizes to its new fuel source. Newcomers will have a difficult time concentrating, but the more you use this diet the less acute the symptoms become. The body becomes more accustomed and comfortable in ketosis with every cycle. The first time I truly went into ketosis, I forgot everything. Worse than usual even. Another symptom that will be hard not to notice is how activities you normally performed with ease become harder. Pushing objects and even mild cardio like riding a bicycle cause limbs to burn within the muscle. This is normal. Your muscles have no food, what we know as glycogen, so they will tire out easily. The sensation of "muscle burn" is actually good - it's a signal you're getting a mild growth hormone response. Being in a carb depleted state means being primed for a lot of cool hormonal activity we would otherwise blunt if we were eating carbs. Goes to show insulin is an extremely powerful anabolic mechanism, but it likes to work alone. All other metabolic processes like fat burning are shut down as long as insulin's large and in charge.

You Tube

Title: **Induction Flu: Signs of Progress or Problems**

Tags: Atkins Diet Weightloss Induction Flu Dieting Carbohydrate Fitness Nausea Dizziness Lethargy Low Carb Bowulf fat obesity

From: bowulf

DAY THREE TO FIVE: After three days of self-monitoring and careful adherence to your macro nutrient intake, you will no doubt be in downtown ketosis. You'll likely be preoccupied with carb counts and weight loss. Carbs are hidden pretty much everywhere, and it will be an educational experience learning which of your favorite foods are "safe" and which ones are not. Most experience a suppression of appetite, but some may actually feel an increased appetite. Go ahead and eat, but stay away from carbs. Somehow, I did this without any noticeable fat gain whatsoever. In ketosis, the body manages to assimilate fat and preserve muscle tissue like no other non-steroidal treatment. That being said, I'll admit I don't understand all the mechanisms behind this metabolic magic. The body God gave us is truly a masterpiece of design and function, and continues to surpass mankind's expectations and comprehension.

STILL ON DAY THREE: You need to start eating vegetables on the third day of the ketogenic phase. Unless you've been living on the planet Zenn-La for the past mega annum (you're excused if your name is Silver Surfer), you're aware fruits and vegetables are important to our health and well-being... and scientists are uncovering more benefits all the time. California mix is fine (although carrots have a bit too much sugar for some perfectionists). Just make sure to douse it in butter to keep fat calories up and maintain ketosis. If you're longing for crisp green granny apple to shine your teeth too, go ahead. Eat some fruit, but either add whip cream to maintain ketosis (you've got an outside chance) or go for a run to deplete liver glycogen again (you still get to keep the vitamins and enzymes of the fruit though).

VEG OUT ON THE KETO-FU

If you *are* firmly planted in ketosis (and you will know it), a salad won't disrupt your flow. When your body's in that incredible metabolic state we know as ketosis, it will happily use both low glycemic carbs and fat as fuel (besides, fibrous green vegetables can't be utilized for energy like traditional carbs). A little caveat: iceberg lettuce is not the dark green fibrous vegetable I've been referring to. It's empty calories and will readily convert to glucose if too much is eaten.

The money line is this: spread out your carbs throughout the day - with protein and fat - and don't eat too much at one time. Try not to exceed 500 calories per meal, but you should know your body best.

DIARY OF A MAD DIETER

I've included a three-day diary outlining everything I ate, my activities during this time, and even how I felt, presented in a "as it happens", first person narrative. I didn't go as far as count calories or micro-manage macro nutrients. That stuff drives me nutters and I've gotten pretty good at estimations and approximate quantities over the years anyhow. I hope it helps.

DAY ONE

At the cruel and ungodly hour of 5AM, so begins my quest in earnest for the weight watcher's holy grail known as ketosis. I stumble groggily to the kitchen and survey my options. Option A: I can have a glass of glutamine dissolved in water, 1000 mg vitamin C and some desiccated liver tablet to take my body out of a catabolic state (ah yes, desiccated liver tablets. Liver tabs dispense a quick hit of muscle-rescuing protein, but with practically zero caloric footprint). You could substitute the liver tablets for a serving of whey protein if that's what cashes your money order.

If maximum muscle gains are the prime objective, a moderate to high carbohydrate diet is ideal. Ketogenic-based diets in-and-of-themselves are not mass makers. However - that pearl of wisdom aside - the ketogenic diet is extremely anabolic when good fats are the focus and it's cycled with the "Freakender" carb-load (described in the "Now You're Playing With Power" chapter), which muscle-building effects are second only to hardcore steroids. And you're reducing body fat to boot, which is very hard to do with any other eating regiment.

Where was I? Oh yes, ways I can exhume my brain dead corpse so early in the morning. Another option is a cup of hot chocolate, but this is a keto-friendly version. I use straight-up cocoa powder with Stevia, the natural low calorie sweetener. I'll add a high-fat milk product (table crème is best) because fat is my friend now. This way I can arouse my faculties with the awesome neurological kick chocolate offers without sugar or taking any harsh and potentially unsafe thermogenics. Once I'm feeling awake and energized, I'll do 30 minutes to an hour of cardio. This is critical to boosting metabolism and achieving ketosis in a timely manner.

6:15AM already? I'll eat again, whether I'm hungry or not. Eating regularly, however small the portions, keeps the fires of the metabolism burning hot! I'll scarf down a few strips of back bacon with eggs and a few tablespoons of hemp oil. I wash it down with *ye olde fashioned* tap water and one to two tablets of Acidophilus Bifidus for healthy digestion. It's also an optimal opportunity to take a multivitamin and a ZMA stack. Btw: you could easily substitute the bacon and eggs for a low-carb protein shake and some flaxseed oil. It's your stomach.

It's 7AM and work at the factory starts. I've got an emergency can of herring or sardines in the back pocket of my coveralls and some beef jerky for a snack a little later. I also got a bottle of water back there (I got big pockets). To be successful at ketogenic dieting, you need to be prepared and you need variety.

8:30AM and my stomach says it's snack time. A measly can of herring can seem like an insult to the stomach so early in the morn, but I've got a hunger on and herring in hot sauce is a fave. I also take a few swigs of hemp oil from the fridge to keep my fat percentage up.

First break is 10AM. I'm eating European-style sausage sticks in the cafeteria with my co-workers, who all have their faces buried in Rubbermaid bowls of cereal. One of my buddies will crack a remark. Yep, I can see his gums flapping' now. They're baffled as to how I eat high-fat foods and stay in shape. I think the irony of eating fat to be lean is too much for them.

12:30PM: Lunch consists of tuna and a high-fat ranch dressing. A co-worker asks me about what I'm eating and feigns interest as I explain it, then goes back to his newspaper.

1:30PM: I've been drinking water throughout the day. Helps me feel human despite the lack of sleep and all the fat I'm eating. Mentally, I'm focused. I make peace with the locust and the cauliflower.

2:30PM: I'm about an hour or so from my daily resistance training, so now's the time to eat a can of oysters for a generous testosterone boost. By the time I get to the gym I'm like a snorting moose in heat (or something like that). Alternately, I may wait till I get home circa 3:20PM and have a quick fruit and protein smoothie before I start bangin' weights, that way nutrients and energy will lend me enough power in the gym so I don't embarrass myself. Tropical fruits like Pineapples, Mangoes and Kiwis are best, because it's quick energy and loaded with vitamins and enzymes to facilitate the digestion of all the protein I've been eating. So here it is: the absolute best time to sneak fruits and other carbs into a ketogenic diet is immediately before strenuous activity like resistance training.

3:30PM: If building muscle is the priority, then I will bring two workout drinks with creatine. One for the first half of my

workout for much needed energy and to load up the muscles with glycogen and a post-workout drink for immediately after to again load the muscles with glycogen and creatine. If fat burning is the theme of the day, I only bring a post workout drink. I make sure the creatine and transport mechanism (be it maltodextrin, dextrose or plain table sugar) is in warm water so it's completely dissolved for easy adsorption into the body. Taking Desiccated Liver Tablets is a good idea, especially if you want a good "pump".

It's 5:00PM and I'm done training. I have my post-workout drink and vitamin cocktail which looks like this:

POST-WORKOUT DRINK:

5g creatine

500mg taurine (optional)

100-250mg alpha lipoic acid (optional)

Whey protein (optional, as you can take that a half hour later with 10-15g glutamine)

A creatine transport system, which is a fancy term for something sugary. 45g Maltodextrin or dextrose is perfect, table sugar is good too. Almost anything that will quickly raise insulin levels and catapult that muscle food, with exception to honey (which will sustain high insulin levels longer than needed) and fruit juices (a big no-no) because fructose will restore glycogen to the liver first, then the muscle, and will prevent you from getting back into ketosis quickly.

VITAMIN STACK:

1000mg vitamin C and/or 30-60 mg grape seed extract

800-10,000 U.I. of beta carotene

400-800 U.I. vitamin E

50-200mcg Selenium

550mg potassium

1 Multivitamin

1000mg or more of brewers yeast. Why brewers yeast? Because it has chromium and helps shuttle more glycogen into the muscle than if you didn't take it. High insulin levels help it work more effectively, so now is the time to supplements with it. In fact, all of these vitamins (with the exception of vitamin E) are best absorbed with a post-workout drink because they're water-soluble and absorb directly into the blood stream where insulin can priority deliver it.

5:30PM: Resistance training should always be followed up with some carbohydrates to restock muscle glycogen even if you're on the Keto-Fu Diet and want to get back into ketosis. Just make the meal small (300 – 500 calories max) and easily digestible (white rice with sugar comes to mind) and then resume your high-fat diet once your stomach feels empty and you're hungry again. If you had fruit before you went to the gym, no worries, it should be completely burned off. Go and have some hi-gly to facilitate muscle recuperation, but keep portion size honest.

8:00PM: Depending on how intensely I'm dieting, I may or may not have whey protein with a shot of hemp oil to balance out my fat to protein ratios. No calculator or ketostix needed for me. I just go by how my body feels. If using ketostix feels right for you (it can sometimes be a motivating factor or educational tool), go right ahead.

10:00PM: I'm worn out and ready for a bedtime story. I'll take a ZMA stack with a glass of glutamine dissolved in water. If insomnia is an issue, I'll take 3mg melatonin – a safe and natural way to induce sleep (provided you don't take it every evening) . If packing on muscle is a priority, I will wake up several times to eat, whether it be simply a whey protein drink or a hardboiled egg (jubilation for the taste buds it is not, but it conforms to the ketogenic diet). I try to keep it calorie light and with no carbs.

DAY TWO

5:30AM rushes up like an all-star running back. Last night my dreams were vivid and jarred me awake, a classic symptom of ketosis. I put the kettle on and make some cocoa powder and Stevia (sans milk or crème). I'll be promptly and briefly kicked out of ketosis, but being in ketosis 24/7 is unrealistic (albeit possible) anyway.

6:30AM: I cycle to work with rock tunes kicking' in my ears for the much needed adrenaline. It's about a 30 minute ride going fairly hard which should re institute ketosis, if I ever had it in the first place. Oh yeah, just before I leave I had a shot of hemp oil and a few desiccated liver tabs.

It's 7:30AM, I'm at work and it definitely feels like my brain is in ketosis. This is not entirely accurate however, since I've read somewhere that it can take a week or longer for the brain to be fully converted from glucose onto ketones. What I'm experiencing is likely ketones being introduced to the mix, and the brain is saying "Eww! What'd you put in my food, fool?! I also have a hint of flu-like symptoms, as if I'm coming down with something. Despite this, I eat some cheese.

I'm pushing bins around at work and it's obvious I don't have my usual "pepper". Every physical Endeavor seems to require more effort and take more out of me. I look at the clock and it's only 8:15AM. I sneak to the cafeteria fridge and have a swig of hemp oil. Yum (not!).

9:30AM and I'm feeling very Zen. I taste the acetone on my breath but I won't chew sugarless gum (sweetened with the dangerous neurotoxin Aspartame). A cinnamon stick would do the trick, if I had one. Instead, I'll drink copious amounts of the filtered water here at work and avoid making out with anyone ;)

It's the 10AM break, and although I'm not even the slightest bit hungry, I eat three eggs with mayonnaise (and a multivitamin) out of a sense of obligation to my muscles and to maintain a positive nitrogen balance. Frequent grazing is also good for the metabolism. Still, it makes me think how often we eat for the wrong reasons, when we're not even hungry. My eldest daughter once wisely remarked "we often eat many more calories than we need to survive". I ponder the truth of that statement often.

Today, at 10:45AM, my mind is as still as stone and I'm completely in the moment. I want to sit in the lotus position under a big tree and meditate, watching every moment blossom into another one. I'm also probably dumb as a doorknob, but despite an unsettled feeling in my stomach, I feel good.

11:30AM: I really should be drinking more water. I lack "zip", but other than that, I feel great. I make a trip to the bathroom and wash my face and hands. I notice my face doesn't look so puffy. Before I go back into the very bowls of hell for another several hours of pure industrial enjoyment, I drink a glass of unflavored Metamucil (the orange stuff has Aspartame, which is a known neurotoxin).

1PM: I'm busy and in the moment. Hustle n' flow.

2PM: I reluctantly eat a can of tuna drenched in ranch salad dressing, and follow it up with two Greens+ caps and a multi. Vitamins have an assuring psychological effect, because you're theoretically covering the gaping holes in an eating regimen such as this. But I'm not naive to the fact vitamins can never replace fresh whole foods.

5:00PM: By the time I do the email thing, check my phone messages, read Slashdot, it's almost 5ish when I hit the treadmill. Before I left the house I took these supplements:

1000 mg vitamin c,

Apple cider vinegar

Desiccated Liver Tablets for the substance and the amino acids for muscle preservation

Zinc

...and I wash it down with some Histamine dissolved in water. It gives me a good boost of energy and I run for an hour.

7:00PM: Dinner consists of ground beef, 3 eggs, olive oil and I dump a whole lotta cucumber dressing on it for flavor. My appetites large and in charge and I practically inhale the food up my left nostril.

10PM: I drink a glass of glutamine dissolved in water before bed, along with 2 caps Acidophilus with Bifidus to facilitate digestion.

11PM: Tired but can't sleep. I drag my exhausted body to the kitchen and eat 3 hardboiled eggs and salad dressing. My taste buds aren't inspired. I fall asleep about midnight.

DAY THREE

At 5:30AM the alarm clock belches in my ear. I awake after another ketosis-fueled dream-heavy sleep. So far so good with the diet. The key component to this diet - more so that EFA's or protein - is willpower, and lot's of it. Anyway, I'm in full blown ketosis now. I've got the classic symptoms: lethargy, the taste in my mouth like I've just been chewing on a lead pipe, bad breath, feeling flush. I need to feel human before work, so I make some cocoa powder with stevia and use table crème for some fat and the modest amount of protein it provides. The cocoa powder has some carbs, but not enough to matter. It'll be burned off with minimal activity.

7AM and work starts anew (welcome to my nightmare). My stomach is complaining so I eat half a dozen sausage sticks as I'm starting the machine.

7:30AM: Ugh, after eating those sausage sticks, my energy levels drop like [insert obscure comic book reference here] Paste Pot Pete vs. Spider-man (it's the saturated fats and God knows what else they put in those things). This just proves how "good fats" (EFA's in particular) energize the body and clear the mind while other fats seem to rob my energy. But alas. I'll be dragging my sorry butt now.

9AM: I feel like Superman right now... with kryptonite down his shorts. I have no power or lasting energy, and pushing around skids at work make my legs burn as if I'd just done a heavy set of hack squats. On the upside, I've lost a good bit o' weight (10 lbs I'd say), but it's mostly water. I've also noticed I pee a lot more, likely due to the fact I'm a) more vigilant about drinking water regularly and b) my body is devoid of carbohydrates (which retain fluids).

The 10AM break buzzer sounds, and not a moment too soon. On the menu today is canned herring with hemp oil. For dessert I have a couple greens+ tablets, beta carotene and a multivitamin. I think astronauts eat better than me.

11:45AM: In ketosis, it seems thinking in any sort-of emotional context is extra-curricular and unnecessary. Personal problems are of no consequence right now. Certainly, the ketogenic diet is ideal for those who suffer with anxiety disorders, as it quiets the mind so effectively.

It's 1PM and my stomach seems apathetic at the prospect of processing more high fat foods. However, I've got a surprise for it. For lunch I've got California mix vegetables (which consists of broccoli, cauliflower and carrots) swimming in butter. For a source of protein, I "fish" a can of herring in hot sauce out of my big coverall pockets. My compliments to the chef!

3PM: I've been enjoying feelings of peace and wellbeing for the last several hours. Describing my state of mind right now is like dancing to silence. Or a room without furniture. Vacant. I feel good though, and work is mercifully over. I get to go home.

With my energy levels so high and no feelings of hunger whatsoever, I head off to the gym for some weight lifting - circa 4PM. Immediately afterwards I drink a post-workout beverage and feel my muscles greedily soak it up. The hit of sugar will stimulate the metabolism too.

5PM: Dinnertime consists of garlic kabasa and a spinach cucumber salad in olive oil. The kabasa I bought on my way home from the gym. The sausage was smoked earlier today and is still warm!

As 7PM rolls around, I eat two bags of dried pork rinds and wash it down with cherry kool-aid sweetened with Stevia, and an hour later I don't feel hella good. Kool-aid consists of a lot of unpronounceable, scientific sounding ingredients, so I toss the rest of it in the trash.

9:30PM: Time to wind down. I drink a glass of dissolved glutamine in water, start a big download on the computer and go to bed.

You Tube

Title: **Eating Low with Amy: Rotel Chicken**

Tags: cooking   amy   von   low carb

cal fat kimkins

From: holababy

ENDING A KETOSIS CYCLE

With all this high-fat intake, low energy levels, burning muscles and nary a Cheeto in sight, you may be asking when the fun starts. Sure, you've lost weight – bad weight – but when can you eat "normal" again? Where's the love? The Keto-Fu diet feels you, my friend. You do not have to be in ketosis all the time to lose weight. In fact, all this low-carbing is most effective (and anabolic) when "cycled" with a high carb, or "Nutrient Loading" phase as we call it. After 5 or so days of extremely low carbohydrate intake, your basal metabolic rate wanes and a fat storing enzyme called lipoprotein lipase will jealously guard the rest of your stored body fat as if it was J Lo at Tiffany & Co. Fat loss comes to a grinding halt. When you stop seeing fat loss results, it's time to increase carbohydrate intake, using high glycemic carbs (cereal, pancakes) and then transition into fruit and vegetables a meal or two later. This is Nutrient Loading in action (Nutrient Loading being one of two approaches and

both are explained in "Now You're Playing With Power") . Your body refuels on the carbs, vitamins and minerals and soon your metabolism will be fired up and ready to lay the smackdown on stored fat again!

Keep in mind, the length of a cycle depends on what you're trying to achieve and the metabolism you have. I advocate anywhere from a 5 to a maximum 10 day ketosis cycle followed by a 48 hour carb-load, but everyone's tolerance to this kind of strict, regimental dieting is different. You may feel completely depleted of energy and willpower after three days in ketosis, in which case it's time for a nutrient loading, even if it's simply a hot chocolate and a piece of fruit, a yogurt smoothie or a bowl of cold cereal for breakfast. Then, when you feel stronger (and hopefully before you start to gain back the fat you've lost), go back to restricting carbohydrates and gradually increase fat intake so to not upset the stomach. Others may be so encouraged by their fat loss, they will continue on to fives days and as long as 10 days (then you're ripe for the *Freakender*).

The other carbohydrate-loading system is called a "glycogen Super compensation carb-load" aka the "Freakender", which is far more dramatic in both application and results, and it's not for everyone. It's used by bodybuilders before a contest, marathon runners before a big race and even boxers and fighters to increase stamina and power. It's downside is that it requires more preparation beforehand, and a rather lengthy full-body workout in a glycogen depleted state (read: grueling) to deplete any last remnants of glycogen and prime muscle storage for maximum adsorption. Glycogen super-compensation carb-loads will also be explained in the next chapter, and you can use either or both carb-loading systems as you see – reluctant pun directly ahead – fit.

REMEMBER...

In ordinary diets, overeating carbs beyond what your body can utilize, results in excessive glucose being stored as fat. Overeating fat however when in ketosis is not a problem. Dietary fats, which are converted to ketones, are simply excreted out the urine when in excess. It's impossible for the body to store body fat when in ketosis.

KETO-FU FRIENDLY FOODS

All these foods are ketogenic friendly and have either no carbs, or such a minute amount it won't even appear on your body's radar. I recommend buying a diverse range of flavorful foods, because this diet can be difficult to stick to at the best of times and variety will help you stay motivated and content. When eating any of the following foods, feel free to add butter, olive or vegetable oil. Do use margarine because it has trans fats (and trans fats inhibit fat loss among other nefarious evil-doings).

ALL VARIATIONS OF EGGS

Whole eggs have nearly a perfect amino acid profile, and the dietary fat concealed within its yoke will provide a stable, slow digesting source of energy. Don't bother with Omega 3 eggs, the extra money you pay for the minuscule amount of Omega 3 isn't worth it. Eat 'em scrambled, fried, deviled, poached or hard or soft boiled. An odd fact: when eggs are boiled, they acquire slightly more carbs (only 1 or 2, but still).

ALL-YOU-CAN-EAT FISH

Salmon, tuna, trout, sardines, mackerel and herring and all shellfish (shrimp, crab, lobster). The last two I mentioned are rich in Omega 3, but I exclude salmon because most of it is fish-farmed and Omega 3 is devoid in their diet.

Herring, on the other hand, is an amazing food. Not only does it have a killer portfolio of healthy fats, including our favorite polyunsaturate Omega 3, but it also has lots of creatine! It's a good source of protein too, albeit fish proteins tend to have a weaker amino acid profile and nitrogen retention than eggs and poultry respectively. It's important to vary protein sources anyway, and fish like this is too valuable to exclude. Fish is also good for all blood types, just ask Namor.

MEAT LOVERS REJOICE!

Red Meat is an important inclusion on the grocery list, especially for bodybuilders that want to add some lean muscle mass while losing flab. Red meat has saturated fats which boost testosterone levels (ok in moderation and in adjunct with an active lifestyle), as well as another kind of fat you may have heard of called conjugated linoleic acid (CLA). CLA helps the body use fat (yes, we're talking body fat) as energy as well as promotes muscle growth. Red meat is also a source of creatine, an amino acid which helps volumes muscle tissue. Pork, Lamb, Ham and Bacon are also viable choices. Note that processed meats, such as ham, bacon, pepperoni, salami, sausages, hot dogs and other luncheon meats may have added sugar and will contribute carbs. Some meats are also liberally seasoned with salt, so drink plenty of water.

FOWL CHOICES

All birds are ideal for the Keto-Fu diet and many bodybuilders swear it's the best protein source for maintaining a highly anabolic state, likely due to it's high nitrogen retention. Chicken, Turkey, Duck, Goose, Cornish Hen are all fine.

GET CHEESY...

and not the low fat kind, my friend. The REAL stuff. Most nutritionists utter a prayer of deliverance every time they pass by the cheddar section, but not us. If you read the macro nutrient ratios on the back, you'll realize it's a near perfect food for the ketogenic diet. It's all protein and fat, with nary a carb. Cheese also has calcium, a mineral we

may be neglecting. And because it's made with slow digesting casein protein, cheese makes a great nighttime snack. Most derivations are included, including cheddar, Mozzarella, Swiss, Cream Cheese, Gouda and goat.

COLD PROCESSED OILS

You'll likely want a variety of oils to choose from, so if you're looking for vegetable oils to dress up a summer salad, make sure it says "cold pressed" or "cold processed" on the label. If not, its healthy properties inherent to Omega 6 have likely been over-processed into oblivion. Olive oil is a good bet.

TREAT YOURSELF

The list is a little shabby, because there really aren't many options for Keto-Fu practitioners who abstain from artificial sweeteners (and artificially sweetened, low-carb foods are everywhere). Use your imagination and experiment. Let me know what you come up with! Try cocoa beans/hot cocoa with Stevia and table crème, or beef and turkey Jerky, pork rinds, but stay away from products like Jell-O light that are loaded with artificial sweeteners. I'll add nuts to the list (almonds, walnuts, sun flower seeds, pine-nuts), but be careful, because these have more carbs in them and can break ketosis if you eat too many.

You Tube Title: **Atkins Induction Acceptable Foods - The Good, The Bad**

Tags: Atkins Diet Weightloss Low Carb Recipes Dieting Carbohydrate Fitness Induction Bowulf obesity fat

From: bowulf

<u>MUSCLE WINS, FAT LOSES</u>

The Keto-Fu diet promotes muscle growth (which is what anabolic means: a "constructive-metabolic state") in a number of ways. When we eat foods rich in Omega 3 and other healthful fats, we accrue the many benefits. Omega 3, over time, makes muscle glycogen stores larger. What happens when your biceps look swole like an overstuffed Thanksgiving turkey? Try it and find out! Muscle glycogen is one of the largest contributors of muscle building, so when you do indulge in carbohydrates, not only is it highly anabolic but more of those carbs will be stored into muscle stores and less into fat cells. High fat diets (along with a low-carb regimen natch) result in a positive nitrogen balance, a precursor to protein synthesis. As you deplete your body of the carbohydrate-derived fuel source glucose, insulin secretion stops and allows other hormones to come into play, most notably testosterone and Human Growth Hormone. Testosterone and Growth hormone response to exercise and even everyday activities is greater when in ketosis, and more often. When muscles are stripped of glycogen, you'll feel an unholy burn doing things you normally would have no problem doing. That lactic burn usually signifies a beneficial hormonal response. It's a good thing.

Conventional diets are extremely catabolic – they destroy muscle as well as fat (fasting is even worse) Ketosis is far more "protein-sparing" or "muscle-sparing", so the hard-earned muscle you acquired in the gym won't be lost with the flab. Tightly controlling our insulin levels will help us maintain and even acquire muscle, as well create ideal conditions for fat loss, which is why carbohydrate controlled, ketosis-inducing diets are so popular with bodybuilders. Even if you're not into resistance training, you need to keep the muscle you've got. Muscle utilizes more calories than fat, ergo more muscle means a faster Basal Metabolic Rate (BMR).

NOW YOU'RE PLAYING WITH
P O W E R

THE CRISIS

Empowered with super human strength and swole muscles by a carb-load gone out of control, you've become a hero wielding a hero sandwich. Bullies used to kick sand in your face, but now you're "the Mac" with the six pack! In a world where rules change like underwear, only you have the power to change your own (rules).

THE PLAN

Unleash the terrible majesty of muscle glycogen super compensation and make the transformation from mere mortal to superhero in a mere 24 hours. Are you ready?

EIGHT GREAT STRENGTH TRAINING FACTS

About had it with the guy who always kicks sand in your face at the beach, and then steals your girl? Of course you are! It's time to stop kicking furniture around in self-disgust and do something about it! The best way to win back your dignity and your woman is to get big and strong with a strength training program. So read this important must-know info first and get lifting!

1. The best strength training programs incorporate major multi-joint, compound exercises, primarily the bench press, the squat and the deadlift. These three are the best exercises for building strength

and muscle, bar none. However, for variety, you can incorporate other highly effective like the ones below:

Shoulders............................... military press

Serratus.................................... skull crusher

Lats...................... underhand cable pulldown

Abdominals.................................... crunches

Thighs...................................... front squats

2. Exercises that isolate small muscles, like the bicep curl, are almost useless when trying to build overall strength.

3. You need to rest a worked muscle group until it is not sore, which is usually two to three days. You also need to rest your entire body for at least 24 hours after a workout.

4. Whilst on a strength training program, eat plenty of quality calories, including carbohydrates. It's no time for low-carb dieting, or dieting of any kind for that matter.

5. Don't go super heavy with the weights all the time, and don't always use the same tempo for lifting and lowering weights. After three heavy days, take an extra day off to prevent overtraining. You can develop explosive power and lift more weight by pushing the weight quickly, but always lift with complete control.

6. Switch up your program every four to six weeks, be it a change in rep scheme, exercise volume or a change in the exercises themselves. Your body will get wise to the "same ole, same ole", which will result in a halt in progression, otherwise known as a plateau.

7. Exercise each muscle group once a week. For example, don't avoid working the legs unless you still feel soreness from the last workout.

8. Any gains in strength, especially in the first month of training, will be almost exclusively due to the increased neurological efficiency and synergistic recruitment of the body as a whole. Long term plums of strength training include increased bone density, better balance and coordination and a higher metabolism due to more muscle.

You Tube

Title: **Core Strength and Fitness Training the HARD way**

Tags: strength training bodybuilding powerlifting exercise performance martial arts plyometrics wrestling football athletic

From: betougher

MUSCLE BATTERY JUICE

Like North Koreans stores weapons of mass destruction in silos for their day of world annihilation (fat chance with you around), insulin stores glucose and fructose in muscle cells or the liver, in which it's then called glycogen. Muscle glycogen not only serves as fuel for those biceps you were beating on with hammer curls earlier, but helps recuperation and the rebuilding of the muscle fibers. Think muscle glycogen as the "stuffing" that gives those biceps more size, and the cavities where insulin tucks away the muscle food as muscle glycogen storage. Any surplus glucose (and especially fructose) not claimed by some bodily process is converted to fat in a process we all fondly remember as phosphofructokinase. Interestingly enough, it takes less insulin to drive glucose into fat cells than muscle cells, which is probably why fruit has such a bad reputation among dieters.

However, I'm not trying to vilify fruit or insulin. Insulin is not the enemy, and it's not responsible for making us fat. Over-eating and improper food choices are the cause of fat storage. Insulin is of utmost importance for overall development of the body - we need this powerful and anabolic hormone to build and repair muscle and distribute the energy we need to function. But anything over and above is stored as fat. Satisfying cravings for sugary foods begets more cravings for sugary foods, ad infinitum. It's easy to see how our weight can get out of control.

The Keto-Fu ketogenic phase is about tightly controlling when and how much insulin is secreted because we aim to build muscle and lose the lard, a tricky but very possible proposition.

You're probably wondering why you're learning this stuff. Ketogenic fat loss "hacks" are generally based on a carbohydrate-restrictive diet, right? For the most part, but swearing off carbohydrates like a pack of cigarettes on New Years Eve is neither a realistic goal nor what we're trying to achieve. Carbs are not evil, but they are overly plentiful in our foods.

Here's a likely scenario. After a workout, when we desperately need insulin's services to uptake and store glycogen into the muscles we just trained, we eat high glycemic foods. These are foods that our digestive processes can convert quickly to glucose so that insulin can divvy it up to hungry muscle cells. White bread is a high glycemic food (and has the nutritional value of a serviette, but that's beside the point), raisins (a better choice) also rank high on the GI. For a majority of the day however, The Keto-Fu Plan is all about the low glycemic foods: fatty fish, cheese, dark green vegetables with olive oil. Low glycemic foods digest slowly and provide your body with a steady stream of energy so you're not repeatedly running into the arms of the Frigidaire like a jealous lover. Yes, high fat, no

carb meals satisfy longer. Fatty foods take longer for the digestive system to assimilate, and that's why you'll notice you're satisfied longer than after a carbohydrate-based meal. This means your stomach won't be nagging you incessantly. You can go on with your life and not have the diet a major preoccupation. And, these low GI foods allow you to burn fat. High insulin levels inhibit fat loss. On the contrary, it encourages fat gain!

CHEAT WITH CARBOHYDRATES

Studies shows consuming a diet high in omega 3, and supplementing with high dosages of vitamin E (900 IU), increases glycogen storage in the muscles. Larger glycogen stores means ingested carbohydrates (even junk food) are more likely to be converted into energy at some point then deposited into the belly bank. To help insulin shuttle more glucose into muscles, take glucose regulating supplements chromium (200 mcg) and apple cider vinegar along with your meal. Toxicity is unlikely, even with higher dosages of chromium (as it is doesn't absorb easily and often gets lost in the urine) but keep dosages within 200 mcg and never exceed 1000 mcgs in a given day. And of course, always consult your doctor regarding supplements you want to try and already take.

SODIUM MANIPULATION

There's a way to get more detail from your muscles without being shredded to the bone, and that's via sodium loading and depleting. As you may or may not know, sodium is just a fancy word for ye olde table salt, and the process of sodium manipulation is as simple as a "Texas two-step". First step is the sodium load, add salt to everything you eat and drink copious amounts of water. In fact, almost twice as much water as you did before, and does so for two weeks for optimum effect. This lowers the secretion of a hormone called aldosterone which regulates sodium and potassium and balances the body's water stores.

For step two, the sodium depletion phase, return to normal consumption of sodium and water. Stop adding salt to everything and you won't need to make all those extra trips to the washroom either. At this time, the hormone aldosterone will begin to draw water from under the skin in an attempt to restore "normal" levels, which will give you a drier, ultra-muscular look. You can accentuate the look by combining garlic and papaya tablets, which makes for a powerful diuretic.

GLADIATOR IN TRAINING:

A staple food for roman gladiators was barley, which gave them strength and stamina. Barley juice is a drink dense in vitamins and minerals, many times more carotene than carrots, more iron than spinach and in a vitamin c comparison, shows up apples in the worst way.

REFUEL THE MACHINE: NUTRIENT-LOADING

The purpose of Nutrient-Loading is to feed and replenish your body with important nutrients along with "normal" foods you love, and it gives you a boost of strength and energy. Moreover, it's anabolic (meaning it encourages muscle growth), as well as makes the muscles you already have look bigger and badder. I have two different systems for determining when and how to carb up: there's <u>Classic Nutrient-Loading</u> (in its various cycle durations) and the <u>One-For-One Nutrient Load</u>.

<u>CLASSIC NUTRIENT LOADING</u>

The Classic Nutrient Loading system mimics the Cyclical Ketogenic Diet (CKD) and is best for those people whose first priority is fat/weight loss. Muscle muscle building is a secondary priority, due to low-to-non-existence glycogen and energy levels throughout the low-carb phase. There are three approaches to Classic Nutrient Loading:

- If you've been low-carbing it for 2-3 days and wish to nutrient-load, do so for no longer than 24 hours (12 hours of high GI carbs followed by 12 hours low GI carbs) and then re-establish ketosis. This is considered a short or "light" cycle. For example, I started the Keto-Fu diet late Sunday night and stayed in ketosis until Wednesday morning. Then for breakfast I ate a bowl of ice cream (it's best to eat highly-refined, high glycemic foods to break a fast or ketosis, when the body is likely to store the glycogen into muscles and not into body fat) followed an hour later by two bowls of "Go Lean Crunch" fiber cereal with chocolate milk. For the rest of the day I went low glycemic (a whole wheat wrap, string beans, and etcetera) until Friday at noon.

- If you've been in ketosis for 5-6 days (considered a normal length cycle), nutrient load for a maximum 48 hours, or limit it to only a day if you're concerned about gaining body fat. Doing the Glycogen Depletion Workout beforehand is a big-time benefit here, because it allows you to eat liberal amounts of highly-refined, high glycemic foods you normally wouldn't even be allowed to look at. Note: Refer to the Freakend Carb-Load for instructions on how to ace an extreme and highly anabolic version of this! Once your glycogen stores are full (and you can determine this by monitoring your face and abs), your body will start storing fat again. It's time to restrict carbohydrates and start the cycle anew.

- If it's been 10 days or more of strict ketosis, take a breather. You can either do the Glycogen Depleting Workout as described elsewhere in this book along with the almighty Freakend Carb-load (maximum two days) or simply reintroduce whole grains, fruits and dark green/root vegetables into your diet and eat normally (for up to five days) . Remember; employ the Keto-Fu Diet in whole or in part, whenever you feel you need it. Use it to your advantage. Use common sense and listen to your body.

Title: **The Natural Bodybuilding Show - Nutrition**

Tags: the natural bodybuilding show nathan mcauley muscle gain fat loss macronutrients tuition how much to eat

From: TNBS

MUSCLE BATTERY JUICE

ONE-FOR-ONE NUTRIENT LOADING

The One-For-One Nutrient Load resembles the Targeted Ketogenic Diet (TKD) in the fact that the low-carb dieting phases are shorter and "interrupted" more often with the ingestion of carbohydrates. This is ideal for those who have a hard time with low-carb diets or for those who rely on regular infusions of carbohydrate-based energy for their workouts. The One-For-One is also desirous because you can eat fresh fruits rich in phytonutrients and enzymes which studies are showing are critical to good health cannot be denied. It works like this: for every one day either in ketosis (or even trying to attain ketosis) equals one "carbohydrate meal".   No carbs for merely a day? Treat yourself to a pancake breakfast, fast food or maybe a big fruit smoothie, then either get back into low-carb mode or normalize your eating by switching to low glycemic foods. Two days low-carbing it and that's two carbohydrate-based meals of your choosing. Manage five days and you earn yourself five high carb meals... or with aggressive feedings of high glycemic foods every two hours, for two days, it is possible to achieve 15 lbs muscle gain! If you need a step-by-step walk-thru complete with Carbohydrates to Glycogen Conversion Formula, read on to "The Freakender"!

Obviously, the longer and more thoroughly the body is depleted of glycogen, the more "thirsty" for carbohydrates your organs and muscles become. When carbohydrates finally do arrive (and are received with 21 gun salute, marching band, red carpet etc), your body will "super compensate" by storing even more glycogen in the empty stores than normal, much like how your body over zealously stores fat after starvation. The great thing is fat storage itself is minimal, if not non-existent, since the focus is on how bad the body wants glycogen. Now imagine pulling off "The Freakender" glycogen super compensation carb-load: muscles become so stuffed with food they literally look and feel like they're going to pop, and energy and power levels rocket out of the stratosphere. Let's take a look at "The Freakender" and all its glory.

THE "FREAKENDER" CARB-LOAD (BE AFRAID)

Want to look like superman at the beach, or run a local 10k race like Flash Gordon? "The Freakender" Glycogen Super compensation Carb-Load will give you the ultimate advantage. It's a three stage system used by bodybuilding pros right before a competition and top marathon runners before a 26.2. It's the Nutrient Loading phase in its most extreme mutation and taken to its ultimate conclusion. There's no counting calories on "The Freakender" (unless you're so compelled) and no workouts at the gym. Eat and get big, that's it. Watch your muscles swell beyond their normal size and feel your strength multiply.

However, before you go any further, a warning: "The Freakender" is <u>not</u> recommended for dainty little princesses looking to lose five pounds before the prom. The very nature and purpose of the glycogen super compensation glycogen-load is to increase muscle size and make you look bigger and thicker – not a desirable quality for most women. If you want to look smaller, use the Keto-Fu diet and forgo the Freakender. It won't make you smaller, but bigger every time!

There are three stages of "The Freakender" Super compensation Carb-Load.

1) Strict, low-carb dieting, preferably in ketosis. You should be intimately familiar with this stage (you can't achieve glycogen super compensation without it). If you're not, go ahead and read the Keto-Fu diet. Once you've achieved ketosis and want to eat carbohydrates again, return to this chapter.

2) A full-body workout so every muscle is stripped clean of glucose and primed for glycogen super compensation. This glycogen depletion "workout" is a lengthy and quite frankly grueling process. No, wait. After a week of ketosis and low-energy levels, it's more like a bloodbath. Every muscle in your body needs to be exercised to ensure no glycogen is present and every

fiber of your physical being primed for super-compensation. The workout is exhausting and will take at least two hours to complete. An hour or so before the workout, eat a few pieces of fruit to refill your liver glycogen stores (your carb-load afterwards will be more anabolic this way) and give you at least a bit of fuel. Below is a suggested workout which not only attacks every major muscle group in the body but is also highly time efficient.

For example, choose an Olympic bar with a moderately heavy weight that allows you to do french curls for the triceps and also "good mornings" for the hamstrings without switching the weight or even pausing (you might need to lower the rep count on some exercises and raise the rep count on others). You'll find this workout can save you time and keep your heart rate up, giving you an aerobic component to the workout.

ATTENTION! ACHTUNG! WARNING! It's important to note you should not be going to failure or forced reps on any of these exercises. This workout is not designed to break down muscle tissue and stimulate muscle growth, but rather deplete glycogen stores and prime the body for super compensation. Doing too much of a workout will screw up isoforms responsible for regulating glucose transport, thereby impairing super compensation, so take those plates off that bar!

Note the format. It's bodypart first, followed by the prescribed, time-saving exercise.

W/ OLYMPIC BAR (MODERATELY HEAVY):

TRAPEZUIS (TRAPS) / behind the back barbell shrugs.

MEDIAL DELTOIDS (MIDDLE SHOULDERS) / military press.

FOREARMS / wrist curls

BICEPS / bicep curls

TRICEPS / French curls

LATISSIMUS DORSI (LATS) / barbell rows

BICEPS FEMORIS (HAMSTRINGS) / good mornings

W/ DUMBBELL (MODERATELY HEAVY WEIGHT):

GASTROCNEMIUS (CALVES) / standing calve raise.

SERRATUS / skull crusher.

W/ TWO DUMBBELLS (MODERATELY HEAVY):

LOWER PECTORALIS / declined press.

MIDDLE PECTORALIS / flat bench press.

UPPER PECTORALIS / incline press.

WITH TWO DUMBBELLS (LIGHT):

POSTERIOR DELTOIDS (REAR SHOULDERS) / inclined rear deltoid lateral raises

INTERIOR DELTOIDS (FRONT SHOULDERS) / lateral raises.

WITH 45 POUND BAR (AND MODERATELY LIGHT WEIGHT):

QUADRICEPS, BICEPS FEMORIS / squats

QUADRICEPS / front squats.

TRAPEZIUS, LOWER BACK / deadlifts

<u>NO WEIGHTS OR EQUIPMENT REQUIRED:</u>

RECTUS ABDOMINIS / crunches

3) Aggressive feedings of highly refined, sugary foods at least every two hours. You just worked off every last vestige of glycogen in your body and primed every muscle for super compensation. Time is of the essence now, since muscle glycogen synthesis is most rapid for the first six ours after exercise (even without a significant insulin response). Before eating any solid foods (re: donuts, cereal or any other simple carbs), drink at least a few post-workout protein drinks loaded with creatine and glutamine to capitalize on the body's heightened state of glycogen synthesis and to enhance muscle growth and recuperation. Drink the first one slowly because the intense sugar rush may make you nauseous.

I documented an earlier carb-load, so I'll use myself as an example. Hopefully from this synopsis you can learn from my mistakes, successes and thoughts.

<u>DAY ONE</u>

It's <u>5AM</u> and I eat a small fruit salad to refill liver glycogen. I follow it up with a glass of glutamine water. I'm totally jacked about the fact I can eat normal today. Yea, super-normal in fact!

At <u>7AM</u> I book it to the YMCA and begin my glycogen-depletion workout. I've got an important appointment at 9:30 which requires me to finish my workout, drag my tired butt home to get dressed in a suit, then jet to my appointment, all within 2 and a half hours. I pulled it off because the weight room was completely empty for over an hour, which allowed me to rush around like a maniac, lifting weights here, checking something else off my list and rushing there to pound out another set. Only one guy sauntered in near the end of my epic, yet slightly abbreviated Freakend workout. His eyes were still blearily from sleep - and he promptly went back to the change room to use the toilet. During my workout I drink a bottle of

glutamine water and supplement with about a dozen desiccated liver tablets for the hit of protein and amino acids.

9AM and I'm done the workout. I slam dunk (with authority) the first of five post-workout beverages, and feel fine despite the reckless disregard for my digestive system. Each of the five post-workout beverages consist of 30 grams protein powder with 2 scoops of this stuff called Glycocarb containing Alpha Lipoic Acid and lots of Maltodextrin for maximum muscle uptake. Total carbs per drink: almost exactly 100 gms.

11:30 AM: After about a time period of roughly two and a half hours between finishing my workout and my fifth post-workout drink, I hit the cereal HARD. I gots me a big box of Raisin Bran with about a dozen 1 liters of Skim Chocolate milk (both were on sale) and I "went to town". Every 2 hours, in fact, more frequently than that did I go to said town. Instead of using the glycogen super compensation formula prescribed below (I hate counting carbs and calories), I simply eat until I'm content.

DAY TWO

I regards to glycogen-load days, I have one, all-important word you must know: Beano. Make sure you have it ready.

The gastro-intestinal discomfort from force-feeding so many high-glycemic carbs into my digestive system has kept me

146

on or near my throne all afternoon. The fiber of the Raisin Bran is in full effect now, and the coarse grains don't always pass through so gracefully if you know what I'm saying. All-in-all, a lot of "uploading" and "downloading" today.

It wasn't so bad Saturday morning. I felt very strong and my muscles were full and tight, so I felt compelled to hit the gym. I overate badly during this Freakend so I wanted to whip up my metabo a bit and burn some calories just to combat some of the fat I might have been storing. Normally, any resistance or cardio training during a Freakend is discouraged (as it fritters away some of the stored glycogen), but you'll feel so strong you might do so anyway. I did incline barbell and dumbbell presses, traps and shoulders and I was lifting very heavy without any fatigue.

I'm not a vain person, not really, but I look pretty dang buff in the mirrors today. Hear me now and believe me later, dis is not a toomah! The Keto-Fu diet/Freakend is a real blast if you like to see yourself in various states of thinness and muscularity. Body recomposition at its best folks!

DAY THREE

I've realized something important upon the completion of my first ketogenic week. Firstly, the 48 hour carbload phase takes every bit as much discipline as the ketogenic phase. I have a hard time holding back during those 2 days, and although it's anabolic to fill your glycogen stores to the point of bursting, there will almost always be a fat spillover which kind of defeats the point of the whole thing. But the amount of weight I gained since Friday was staggering. I weighed 188 on Friday and on Sunday night weighed in at 201, so I packed on 13 lbs in just two days. The amount of fat that I gained was modest. It appears I've added an extra layer of skin on my abs, not bad considering the obscene volume of high glycemic food I consumed lately. If only I could hold back, or shorten the carbloading phase to just one day. Maybe doing a split on the Saturday would help negate some of the access glucose I was producing, and allow me to eat as aggressively as I did. I think that once the novelty of the carbload wears off, I'll be more sensible about it, and I'll see more profound and lasting fat loss.

CARBOHYDRATES - GLYCOGEN CONVERSION

There's a formula we can use to induce how much of this junk food we're inhaling will be converted to muscle glycogen before there's a real chance of it being stored as fat. It's not exact, and it's a little subjective because you determine how depleted of glycogen your body is, but it's a good guideline to be conscious of. It goes a little something like this: a healthy, exercised body with good insulin sensitivity can synthesize muscle glycogen anywhere from 10 millimoles (mmol) per kilogram (remember 1 kg equals 2.2 lbs) per hour (hr) to 15 mmol/kg/hr - *for the first 24 hours*. Actually, the studies relating to the conversion and expending of glycogen are so numerous and the data so staggeringly vast, you can find numbers significantly higher and lower due to route of administration, the exercise performed and an infinite other variables, but I've decided to round the numbers and not get too extreme either way.

I've made it easy. Select a number from 10 to 15 for what most accurately describes your dieting and workout efforts in preparation for glycogen super compensation and punch

that number into the formula. 10 represents a rate of 10 mmol/kg/hr of muscle glycogen replenishment, and you would choose this if something went "wrong" in the process:

- You either didn't perform a full body workout (but rather worked on one of two major muscle groups)

- Low-carbed for only 3 days.

- Sub-maximal water intake during workout and glycogen replenishment. About 500 ml of water is required per gram of muscle glycogen stored.

- Didn't use insulin agonist's ala chromium, apple cider vinegar, brewers yeast or vanadium (vandal sulfate) to assist in glycogen uptake.

Choosing 15 mmol/kg/hr would indicate you went to the max:

- You performed a full-body glycogen depletion workout

- Drank lots of water

- You were in ketosis for 3-5 days

- Used insulin agonists to improve glycogen super compensation rates

Choosing 12 to 14 would be a variance between the two extremes I described.

For the super compensation weekend I documented earlier, I was 72 kg in lean body weight. I chose 15 mmol/kg/hr because I'm so very hardcore, and that equates to 15 grams of carbs that can be converted to muscle glycogen for the first 24 hours after the grueling 2 hour glycogen-depleting workout. Excessive eating above and beyond other energy expenditures and physiological processes will likely result in body fat

15 X 72 = 1080 grams of carbs, eaten every 2 hours. (1080 / 12) equals 90 grams of carbohydrates per meal. Each gram of carb is 4 calories, so (1152 X 4) is a whopping 4608 calories of carbohydrates exclusively.

SUPERCHARGE YOUR STRENGTH SIX WAYS, RIGHT AWAY!

Yes! There are ways you can increase your strength, beyond normal, right now or within the next few minutes. And no, it does not require radiation, chemicals or toxic waste:

1. Research has revealed that those who supplement with caffeine enjoy an increase in upper body strength, and perform 2.1% better than their previous one rep maximum. Unfortunately, caffeine is an addictive substance which can do more harm than good, so I'll suggest theobromine (a bitter alkaloid of the cacao plant and found in abundance in dark chocolate) as a reasonable substitute. It should have the same strength boosting benefit as caffeine, but without the jarring, depleting effect of the synthetic stuff.

2. Women have a way of inspiring men to do ridiculously stupid and machismo acts to garner their attention, and you can use their uncanny ability to your advantage to summon unchartered entrepots of power. You'll need to find where they populate and be there. Why do you think the gym

3. is so busy at 6-8 pm weekdays? It's not merely because people are off work!

4. Crank your favorite rock out, head banger music and ride the adrenaline kick! Adrenaline, aka Epinephrine is the "fight or flight" hormone, which, when discharged into the blood stream, boosts the supply of oxygen and glucose to the brain and muscles and elevates blood sugar levels for easy energy conversion. Coordinate your heavy lift with the most triumphant hook in the song and you'll be surprised how much you can heft.

5. Within the revered inner sanctums of the know, there is an effective strength-increasing tactic called "Enhanced Neural Drive". It's a method of psyching-out your central nervous system by executing a single lift of your one rep maximum. Once you've lifted what you feel is your maximum weight, or even attempted it, your body will expect another ultra-heavy load for the next lift, and thus recruit every last nerve and muscle. Your next lift (a lighter weight, but still heavier than normal) will be surprisingly effortless.

6. You're only as strong as your weakest link, and with lifting straps, you can say goodbye to failing grip strength, the weakest link that prevents you from realizing your superhuman capacity and fully overloading larger upper body muscles.

7. A Mediterranean meal consisting of whole wheat pasta, dark leafy vegetables and olive oil. No, I'm serious. The pasta will refill glycogen stores and provide muscles with long-burning fuel, the vegetables provide nutrients, antioxidants and enzymes, and the mono saturated fat of the olive

oil will jack your testosterone levels to the moon, thereby increasing your strength.

FLEX WITH FRUCTOSE

If you're a bodybuilder on the five day low carb, 2 day carbload Keto-Fu cycle, you'll want to hold up on the fruit intake. Fructose converts to liver glycogen and any spillover converts to fat: it isn't hastily shuttled up the blood stream and into muscles like glucose. You want to achieve maximum cell volumization, so stick with the cereal and skim milk and eat fruit sparingly, or save it for a post-workout energizer.

The trick is eating a moderate amount; say one or two servings, shortly before training. Fructose (the sugar in fruit) converts to liver glycogen and any spillover goes directly to the big ole' booty: it isn't shuttled up the blood stream and into muscles like glucose.

How do I get back into ketosis? Strip the liver clean of glycogen with 30 minutes to an hour of cardio. You like cardio right?

GET THE KUNG-FU GRIP

Good grip strength and a firm handshake has always been the calling card of the confident and powerful. To wit: the archetypal Renaissance man Leonardo Da Vinci was known to unbend horseshoes and mangle metal with his bare hands. Movers, shakers and the big money makers all express greeting with a direct stare in the eyes and a firm handshake. A limp-wristed response will never impress anyone.

Get a firm grip on the situation. Understand there are different parts of the body that contribute to superhuman hands (fingers and thumb, palm, wrist and forearm), as well as distinct and separate aspects of hand strength (crushing, pinching and supporting). Here's how to get that kung-fu grip that says you're for real:

- For Gripping Strength, try towel wringing. You'll want to soak a big bath towel that your hands can barely get around, and wring it like it was the devil's neck. Rinse and repeat (Thank you, you're a great audience. I'm here all night. Try the veal). Torsion spring grippers are also effective at building grip strength, but if you want real power and not merely capable of lame party tricks like crushing beer cans, you'll need to step up to the Captains of Crush® Grippers found at IronMind.com.

- Pinching Strength is the ability to hold object(s) using only the compression force of your finger(s) and thumb. Pinching plates is an effective exercise. Pinching pennies is not.

- Supporting Strength is used anytime you carry a suitcase, heft a bucket of water or drag a defeated supervillian to the police. A few solid hours volunteering at the local food bank is a great way of "supporting" strength!

- Wrist and Forearm Strength is as important as hand strength, and can be improved using the weaver stick lift and barbell wrist curls (palms up and down). Do these exercises until the burn gets so bad the fire alarm goes off.

The best way to develop the kung-fu grip and superhuman hand strength is by helping up somebody up who is down and out. Look for people in need of your help - don't let an opportunity slip through your fingers!

Title: **Kettlebell flips, Stone Pinching, and Grip Strength Training**

Tags: strength training bodybuilding powerlifting exercise performance martial arts plyometrics wrestling football sports

From: betougher

STACKING UP THE EVIDENCE

THE CRISIS

Withheld information, nebulous answers, suspect products, poor results, confusion and lies – welcome to the dietary supplement industry!

THE PLAN

It's highly classified information for your eyes only! We take you deep within our top secret lab and reveal potent supplement combinations, foods that will unleash uncanny anabolic powers and expose shocking proof of foul play by the FDA! Brace yourself for a thrill-ride full of unexpected twists and turns!

FACTS ON FATS

I'll be first to admit the Keto-Fu Plan is not a celebration for the taste buds, but while some will feel deprived with it's lack of variety, others will revel at the chance to eat forbidden fatty foods and actually lose weight. As a general recommendation, seafood such as cod, mackerel, sardines and salmon are perfect ketogenic-friendly food which are beneficial for all blood types, nations, kindred's, tongues and peoples of the world (including you mister fish-hater).

However, before you jet out the bat cave to KFC to "get shredded out of control", you need to understand not all fats are fair game. Fish oils, we're talking Omega 3 in particular, is best. Your mama was right: fish really are brain food! Essential Fatty Acids (EFAs), as those found in cold-pressed olive oil and walnuts, are also ideal. Saturated

fats are admissible and almost impossible to avoid on the ketogenic diet anyway, but Trans fats are not. Cholesterol is a fat too, but isn't included here because proper adherence to the Keto-Fu Plan and fat ratios will lower bad LDL cholesterol, raise good HDL cholesterol and lower triglyceride counts. Read on for the important facts on fats!

Monounsaturated fats: The name "mono" is the Greek word for "one", after its atom structure which refers to the amount of hydrogen atoms that are bonded to carbon atoms. In this case, a Monounsaturated fat molecule has one double bond. I hope you're taking notes because I'm going to quiz you later.

The most common source of monounsaturated fats is olive oil, and those Italians were right to use so much of it. Along with antioxidant flavanoids, polyphenols and tocopherols antioxidants, oils rich in monounsaturated fats lower bad LDL cholesterol without changing good HDL cholesterol. It protects against lower blood pressure and inflammation, which are also linked to heart disease and a host of other degenerative health problems. The risk of getting diabetes is lessened to boot. Here are some other sources you can find monounsaturated fats:

Canola oil

Peanut oil

Avocados

Olives

Almonds

Pecans

Polyunsaturated fats: Polyunsaturated fats get the name "poly" meaning "many" from its multiple connected carbon atoms and absent hydrogen atoms. It's less healthy than monounsaturated - it lowers bad LDL and good HDL cholesterol - but it regulates inflammation much the same and is good for overall cellular integrity. A distant second to its monounsaturated brethren, polyunsaturated fats are found in plentiful supply on the grocery shelves and in these oils:

Soy

Sesame

Corn

Safflower

Sunflower

Saturated fats: Poor saturated fats. Like Spider-Man who saves the city one issue and becomes public enemy number one the very next issue, saturated fats are misunderstood and maligned. I recently saw a jar of peanut butter which proudly proclaimed on the label: "Low in saturated fats", meanwhile its ingredients list the far more deadly partially hydrogenated oil. This is a very popular brand and people are buying and eating this garbage and thinking they're doing themselves a favor. If meeting God is high on the to-do list, then by all means.

True, saturated fats raise LDL cholesterol levels which in due time can cause heart disease, BUT (note the caps, because this is a mother of a "but") this is under normal dietary conditions. When in ketosis, the body gorges on fatty acids and the very cholesterol that blocks arteries. Dig: your cholesterol levels are very likely to go down on this diet! This may explain why Eskimos (who dine on raw red meat and whale blubber almost exclusively for many months of the year) have staggeringly low cholesterol readings and virtually nonexistent incidences of heart disease. It's also a testament to the amazing healthful properties of Omega 3, something the whale blubber is a rich source of. Moral of the story? Your fat intake should primarily consist of Essential Fatty Acids (EFAs) derived from fish, or move to the North Pole. Dress warm!

One more thing about this unfairly ill-reputed fat. Saturated fat derived from red meat and cholesterol is a precursor to the androgenic hormone testosterone, the very essence of alpha-maleness. Higher T levels mean more fat burning and more muscle building. Man, if Eskimos were into weight training, they'd be one buff bunch!

Beef (CLA is an anti-catabolic, antioxidant fatty acid found in heated beef. It's one of the few good fats).

Butter (butter fat contains short-chain triglycerides, available for quick energy)

Chocolate

Poultry

Palm oil

Coconut oil

Essential Fatty Acids (EFA's): Essential Fatty Acids are classified as polyunsaturated fats, but their benefits far surpass your common salad dressing or even monounsaturated fat like olive oil. As the name would suggest, EFA's are essential to good heart, neurological and insulin functioning, right down to the molecular level, and are the most critical element to the ketogenic diet. There are three types and you probably already know of them:

Omega 3: May also come packaged as alpha-linoleic acid or ALA. It's the core of the ketogenic diet regime, and should be taken liberally. Oils abundant with Omega 3 are not to be cooked with - that would denature the product and render it useless. Serve chilled and add it to salads or your protein drink, or swig it straight from the bottle if you're too macho to use a spoon.

Omega 3, along with the healthful properties already mentioned, help blood glucose levels stay tickity-boo. Your body cannot manufacture Omega 3, you need to supplement with it.

In what would seem like an attempt to confuse you, I'll mention there are a subset of Omega 3's; three of them in fact. They are ALA, DHA and EPA and we'll need to discuss them in further detail a little later. Knowing the variations of Omega 3 will help you be a more informed consumer than someone who overheard a blurb on CNN about Omega 3's remarkable healing powers.

Omega 6: North American's who eat meat and/or eggs from grain fed animals, uses soy, corn, safflower or sunflower oil or any of these oil-based products thereof is likely getting too much Omega 6 in their diet. The proper ratio of 3's to 6's should be 1:1, but most are doing far, far worse than that. Try 20:1. Too much Omega 6's can lower good HDL cholesterol, but by supplementing with ample amounts of Omega 3, you won't need to get into the maddening situation of figuring out 3 to 6 ratios every time you sit down to eat.

Omega 9: Unlike 3's and 6's, Omega 9 can be produced in the body. Peanut and Sesame oil is ultra-rich in Omega 9's also. Omega 9 is imperative for health and well-being, as is 3 and 6, but you need not go out for Chinese food stir-fried in peanut oil every night of the week to keep from falling into an Omega 9 deficit. Focus on Omega 3.

<u>Three Omega 3's</u>: We now know we need to center our attention on Omega 3, but there's a little more to it than that. Some Omega 3's are better than others, although it's better to supplement with any of the three types than none at all. Your brow just furrowed, so I'll explain: Omega 3 can either be derived from plants (ALA) or fish (DHA, EPA), and studies are suggesting the fish-based oils are best. Actually, I've been able to create an amazing thermogenic effect by eating three to five cans of Omega-3 rich fish a day. However, fish haters can rejoice. When sufficient amounts of ALA is consumed (Flaxseed oil is the best source of ALA and should be in every fridge), the human body can produce DHA and EPA. How effectively it does this depends on the age of the individual.

<u>DHA and EPA Sources</u>

*salmon

Sardines

Mackerel

Herring

Anchovies

Halibut

Sea bass

*tuna

Devoid of Omega 3 if fish farmed (this is pretty much anything canned and affordable).

<u>ALA Sources</u>

Flax seed and oil

Canola oil

Walnuts

Wheat germ

Hemp seed

Soybeans

Pursuance

You Tube

Title: **Omega 6 and Omega 3 Fats**

Tags: omega fats dr mercola mercola.com doctor metabolic health diet nutrition natural cure remedy treatment

From: mercola

Tran's fats: Trans-saturated fatty acids, Frankenstein fats, partially hydrogenated oil or shortening - call it by whatever known name you want, but don't put this in your body! Partially hydrogenated oil is polyunsaturated oil with a manipulated hydrogen profile to make it solid and ultra-stable. This ominous yet omnipresent fat can inhibit your fat loss - even in a state of ketosis - and halts muscle growth by neutralizing the adsorption of amino acids! Kinda puts the kibosh on the KFC idea, doesn't it? Its rap sheet continues to get longer and more disturbing as scientific research exposes its many harmful effects. Beware partially hydrogenated and hydrogenated oils and shortenings. It will be listed on the food package's ingredients list, and if these horrible fats are there, avoid and buy something else!

Margarine

Cookies and biscuits

White bread

Chips and nachos

Donuts

Commercial deep fried foods

Diglycerides: a fat derived from soybean, sunflower, or palm oil, are found in many processed foods, from ice cream to gum. Much like Trans fats. It acts as an emulsifier and stabilizer - also much like Trans fats - but Diglycerides (or diacylglycerol as it's sometimes listed in ingredients) can actually promote weight loss. Much un-like Tran's fats!

Commonly, fatty foods like bacon and link sausages are usually shunned in favor of "healthier" foods, but what if you could eat these types of foods from time to time, or even regularly, and not gain weight and not require triple-pass heart surgery at the age of 40? It's all in how we combine our foods! I'll give you a simple rule to remember, but first, let's recap: Carbohydrates are the bodies preferred fuel source. The body can convert foods like rice, fruit and bagels easily to energy. If it's present in the system, it'll choose carbs over fat and protein every time. Protein is a distant second. Your body would much rather use protein (it's the amino acids it really wants) to build and repair muscles. Fat is the least efficient fuel source, and the body will store it away to one of your problem centers unless you engage in activities that will expend huge amounts of calories after that meal of bacon and buttered white bread.

The formulas of food combining are carbs + protein or fat + protein, but never carbs + fat in the same meal. If you want to eat bacon and link sausages, abide by these rules to negate any negative side effects: Eat on an empty stomach. If your digestive system hasn't assimilated its last meal, it's probably not a good idea to eat anyway unless you're a bodybuilder on a bulking diet. Eat protein and fat with nothing else and don't wash it down with orange juice (that's carbs), or home fries (carbs) or any carbohydrates for that matter. Supplementing the meal with Omega 3 found in flax seed or hemp oil is a good idea as studies seems to suggest Essential Fatty Acids like Omega 3 and 6 counteract heart disease. Eskimos live almost exclusively on fatty meats like whale blubber (which is high in Omega 3), and there is a very low incidence of degenerative disease. Always try to keep within the 500 calories range, regardless of what you're eating. Fat has more calories per gram (9) than protein (4) or carbs (4), so keep that in mind when your slam-dunking pork chops down your lungs. Any food not needed for energy will be converted to stored body fat.

FRUIT AFTER A WORKOUT

The liver is a very important organ, and one of its functions is supplying energy to the entire body. When liver glycogen stores are full (merely three, eight ounce glasses of orange juice will fully replenish liver glycogen), an enzyme responsible for signalling the body to store glucose as glycogen, communicates to the body all glycogen stores are full. This of course is wrong, especially if three eight ounce glasses of o.j. are all you've had since weight training! Now, because you've opted to drink a high-fructose beverage first, the chance to refuel tired muscles with glycogen is b0rked and any carbohydrates ate afterwards will be converted to fat!

So what's the lesson to be gleaned from this chilling tale? Opt for grains and starchy foods and avoid eating fruit directly after a workout.

But that's not the end of the story:

THE KETO-FU PLAN AND FRUIT

Although considered sacrilege by ketogenic purists, it can be done, even in mid-ketosis cycle. Its true hard-earned ketosis is broken when you eat fruit, but the payoff is a mother load of phytochemicals (a natural bioactive compound that works synergistically with nutrients to protect against disease) vitamins and enzymes the Keto-Fu Plan is sorely lacking, along with quick energy to kick some ass in the gym. Still, with this cheating comes a penalty. To get back into ketosis requires a process is called aerobic glycolysis (Greek for huffing it). The street term is cardio and is considered a swear word in hardcore bodybuilding circles (speaking it is followed by a spit on the ground). However, only cardio can deplete liver glycogen stores in a timely manner. Sleep and normal activity will eventually do the same, but if you want to get back into ketosis ASAP, cardio is key. Anywhere from 30 minutes to an hour of running on a treadmill should be sufficient.

Weight lifting, on the other hand, employs a different metabolic state called the ATP/CP energy system. It does not utilize oxygen; therefore it's ineffective for depleting liver glycogen unless you do high reps and supersets with little or no rest, thereby making it aerobic in nature. When it's all said and done, have your post workout drink, wait an hour to have a meal and make it of the no-carb / protein / high fat variety.

MORE FACTS ON FRUIT:

Opt for natural and unprocessed foods over man-made processed foods because "In God We Trust". We can't rely on the FDA or a multinational corporation to keep us healthy or even tell us the truth. Their motives are money, not the safety of the consumer. That's why raw fruits and vegetables are best: you don't need to squint at a list of ingredients! Fruit is also an excellent source of energy. What better way to wake up than a piece of (insert your favorite fruit here, mine is pineapple) bursting with flavor and sweetness? Eat a piece of fruit before a workout. You'd break ketosis but fill your liver glycogen, which will in turn transport glycogen to the working muscles groups when needed, thereby building more muscle.

But why the bad rap on fruit, especially among dieters? The problems arise when too much fructose (the sugar in fruit) is consumed. Studies show too much fructose can cause obesity (because fructose so readily is stored into fat cells), and it messes with those hormones insulin, leptin and ghrelin we discussed earlier. Insulin and leptin - the hormones responsible for signaling contentment - are low (re: inactive) after a "significant" amount of fructose is ingested. We'll use a fruit beverage for instance. Ghrelin hormone levels (which stimulates the appetite) tends to elevate and can lead to overeating. These hormones respond more favorably to glucose, thus it's easier for the dieter to push away from the dinner table. A general rule is boost fruit intake to gain weight and increase vegetable consumption to lose weight. More ominous findings show fructose can be a contributing factor in diabetes, heart disease, cancer and accelerate the aging process. So armed with the knowledge that fruit is good but fructose (especially synthesized fructose found in commercial beverages) can be downright bad for you, here are the top 5 fruits with minimal fructose and higher glucose amounts, as well as the top 5 most fibrous fruits you can legally consume without a doctors prescription and a cast iron bung hole.

MOST GLUCOSE LEAST FRUCTOSE RATIO

Number five................................ peaches

Number four................................cherries

Number three........................... nectarines

Number two............................... kiwi fruits

And the number one fruit with the highest glucose/least fructose (with a bullet)....... Blueberries!

Grapes and watermelon are at the bottom of the list and are the least Keto-Fu friendly. Along with the fruit, I recommend supplementing with either creatine citrate or calcium citrate to minimize fat storage and promote glycogen storage.

THE ENEMY IS WITHIN

I have a confession. I was one of many bamboozled into thinking aspartame was good for you. This artificial sweetener (which goes under the brand name NutraSweet), even sounded Nutra-itious. I thought I was doing myself a favor by opting for this synthetic sweetener over real table sugar. I believed with aspartame I was under the radar of my blood glucose levels and avoiding an insulin spike. I naively believed the FDA (Food and Drug Administration) made decisions based on my health and not on money. I was laughably wrong. Nonetheless, I can't blame anyone but myself. I've disputed the nutritional claims of food products before, but I *chose* to believe aspartame was safe. Murmurings of it's toxicity I regarded as speculation and conspiracy from paranoid weirdo's wearing tinfoil hats - *until I became so ill, so poisoned with aspartame* - that I could no longer ignore the truth. NutraSweet/Equal/Spoonful and Splenda are contaminates unfit for human consumption. They are not "healthy alternatives to sugar". They are dangerous neurotoxins: poisonous foreign substance in the brain which causes distressing brain tumor-like symptoms including retinal damage, anxiety, depression, confusion, headaches, forgetfulness and chronic fatigue disorder. The large multinational corporations which marketed aspartame under the   misleading brand name NutraSweet are perpetrating a criminal conspiracy to knowingly harm consumer's health for profit and gain. I truly believe this.

But let's back up a minute. This is what aspartame is: aspartame's scientific name is 1-aspartyl 1-phenylalanine methyl ester, and its composition is 50% phenylalanine, 40% aspartic acid and 10% methanol, the same methanol used for thinning paint wood stains. Most people know methanol is a dangerous toxin. Your local poison control center will be happy to educate you on its devastating effects. Phenylalanine and aspartic acid on the other hand, are harmless amino acids when complimented with other aminos in natural foods. They become dangerous neurotoxins when ingested in isolation. Alone and in high concentrations, they run amuck in the central nervous system, disrupting neuronal synapses, protein synthesis and mutating DNA. It's no wonder aspartame poisoning is so commonly misdiagnosed; you can have a myriad of physical and mental symptoms.

Title: Aspartame, MSG, Dumbing Down Society

Tags: Aspartame   msg   milk   sucralose

From: jonbaum1153

Here's another money line: Avoid anything with isolated amino acids. Only consume foods with at least 8 essential amino acids. Why? Because anything less may cause surpluses and imbalances your body can't properly regulate. NutraSweet is a perfect example.

Let me put it this way: your body doesn't understand these synthetic substances, so it stores these artificial sweeteners in your brain! Artificial sweeteners also screw up insulin regulation, giving you a sugar disorder (if you're waking up in the middle of the night dying for carbohydrates, now you know why). Obviously, you should stay away from any and all of the zillion products with aspartame, including sugarless gum.

So what can we do when your sweet tooth bears its fangs? Check out Stevia, a natural low-carb sweetener used in South America for 2000 years and can be found online and at the local health food store near you. It's low in calories and in carbohydrates (which makes it ideal for ketogenic diets) but on the downside the price is several times higher than table sugar, and you'll find certain Stevia extract products are mixed with a rice maltodextrin "filler". Then there is fruit. Fruits higher in glucose than fructose will satisfy your sweet tooth and give you a "hit" of vitamins... but be aware it will terminate ketosis immediately if you're there. A reader (appropriately nicknamed Catwoman) wrote in to suggest Erythritol, a natural sugar alcohol that is nearly as sweet as refined table sugar but does not affect blood sugar. She even sent a sampling of the fine white powder through the mail to me (which would explain why a man in a trenchcoat is staked out across the street of my apartment building 24/7).

Finally, there's the arch enemy of dieters and diabetics everywhere... the real thing ™: table sugar! It won't give you brain tumors, seizures or destroy your eyesight but what all sugars do (sucrose, fructose and all the seemingly infinite variations) is make you old faster. Sugar accelerates aging, so use in moderation.

You Tube

Title: **Aspartame Danger**

Tags: Aspartame   artificial sweetener   ancer-causing morando soffritti

From: dailyhealthupdates

CRACKING MOTHER NATURE'S COLOR CODE

Mother Nature often speaks in riddles, and there are many things of this world mankind does not understand, but one secret we are beginning to unravel is the color code of fruits and vegetables. Every color represents a different subset of vitamins and phytochemicals that contain protective, disease-preventing compounds. By eating the rainbow of fruits and vegetables and their individual health-promoting properties you're getting much needed variety and broadening your intake of nutrients and enzymes. Here's the list of colors and what they mean:

RED pigmentation on fruits and vegetables indicate lycopene or anthocyanins which may help reduce risk of several types of cancer, especially prostate cancer. Note: you gotta cook tomatoes to unlock its full cancer-fighting properties. Examples of fruits and vegetables in the red group include: red apples, beets, red cabbage, cherries, cranberries, pink grapefruit, red grapes, red peppers, pomegranates, red potatoes, radishes, raspberries, rhubarb, strawberries, tomatoes and watermelon.

GREEN fruits and vegetables are colored this way because of a plant pigment called chlorophyll. Every child's favorite food - broccoli! - contains fiber, carotenoids, calcium and vitamins, A, C and K. Green fruits and veggies are loaded with antioxidants and cancer fighting phytochemicals, so they need not apologize for their boring appearance. Members of the boring but healthy green group include: green apples, artichokes, asparagus, avocados, green beans, broccoli, brussel sprouts, green cabbage, cucumbers, green grapes, honeydew melon, kiwi, lettuce, limes, green onions, peas, green pepper, spinach and zucchini.

Anthocyanins are the BLUE AND PURPLE plant pigments in blueberries, prunes and plums have some of the strongest anti oxidizing properties we know of. They have anti-inflammatory benefits and protect the brain from oxidative damage which causes neurodegenerative diseases. It would seem blueberries and blueberry supplements are the ticket to a healthy mind! Here are representatives of the blue/purple group: blackberries, blueberries, eggplant, figs, plums, prunes, purple grapes and raisins

Carotenoids are responsible for the YELLOW AND ORANGE pigmentation on fruits and vegetables. The beta-carotene found in carrots and sweet potatoes is an immune-booster and cancer fighter, and is particularly important for the elderly. Some of the fruits, while not a significant source of beta carotene/vitamin A, do have plenty of vitamin c. Fruits and vegetables in the yellow/orange group include (again, this is not a complete list): yellow apples, apricots, butternut squash, cantaloupe, carrots, grapefruit, lemons, mangoes, nectarines, oranges,

papayas, peaches, pears, yellow peppers, pineapple, pumpkin, rutabagas, yellow summer or winter squash, sweet corn, sweet potatoes, tangerines, yellow tomatoes, yellow watermelon.

WHITE fruits and vegetables are colored by white pigments known as anthoxanthins. Such healthful properties of these white plants include a natural chemical called allicin, which provides antibiotic properties as well as anti-fungal protection. Bananas and potatoes are also in the white family and yield the mineral potassium. Fruits and vegetables in this group include: cauliflower, garlic, ginger, mushrooms, onions, parsnips, potatoes and turnips.

NINJA IN TRAINING:

A ninja's diet largely consisted of grains (buckwheat), vegetables (fiddlehead, ferns, bamboo shoots and brackens), fruit (dried plums, apricots) and other natural foods dense in vitamins and minerals (like seaweed). Remarkably, despite their raw, macrobiotic diet, they still opened many cans of whoop-ass to any who wanted some.

AMINO ACIDS

"Where's the beef" is the kitsch catch phrase which has long worn out it's welcome in a 1980's Wendy's ad campaign and still continues to rears it's ugly head from time to time, and this unfortunately is one of those times. Yes, with all the growth-promoting hormones, antibiotics, tranquilizers, pesticides, animal drugs, artificial flavors, coloring dyes, industrial wastes, (gasp for air) and other such villain in our beef and other red meats, say nothing of saturated fat (empty calories yes, but not the trumped-up villain it's made out to be), we need to be sparing about our red meat intake.

Luckily, there are other equally important protein sources we can choose from, and from an amino acid standpoint (amino acids being the building blocks of life) eggs are an ideal choice. Amino acid-wise, eggs have a perfect amino acid profile, and are the standard to which all other protein sources are judged. Beef (whose reputation we recently sullied) has 69% of eggs 100% amino acids and cow's milk rates at 60%. Soybeans stand at 47%. Fish – my personal favorite and the protein source ideal for all blood types – is 70%.

There are 9 essential amino acids your body cannot manufacture and must be obtained from food, 22 in total. The trick in getting all amino acids into your diet is to pair up high amino acid foods like whole eggs with low amino acid foods like beans (or by mixing fruit yogurt and tuna together like my friend *shudder*). You can also take amino acid supplements which will ease your worries if your diet is inadequate.

You Tube

Title: **Multi-Source Proteins, Amino Acids, BCAA's**

Tags: bcaa amino acids nutrition supplements protein max muscle diet

From: maxmusclesanmateo

SUPERHERO SUPPLEMENTATION

When we shift into this dynamic new metabolic phase called ketosis, we need to make sure we're addressing health concerns and possible nutrient deficiencies this high fat/low carb diet may present. We'll sneak in most

vitamins/minerals/nutrients with top quality "cheat foods" before resistance training, but we're going to have to rely on supplements to keep our bodies healthy and running in optimum condition.

First and foremost, adequate water consumption cannot be overstressed. High protein, carb-restrictive diets have a diuretic effect on the body. But there is yet another reason to be vigilant about drinking water, and that is because many of the vitamins recommended here are water-soluble (vitamin E is fat-soluble). They break down easiest with ample amounts of H2O and are absorbed directly into the blood stream, so water is mucho important (and when I break out the Spanish, listen up). Warm water is best because it's absorbed quicker into the body (apparently the Chinese have known about this lil' nugget of knowledge for 4000 years). Cold water, on the other hand, requires more body energy to warm before it's assimilated, so if you're looking for a stupid diet trick to burn off an extra couple of calories, there you go.

Ok, now on to specific supplementation, but with the caveat that I am not a doctor and dosage recommendation may vary wildly with the Recommended Daily Allowance (RDA). Consult a professional health practitioner before taking any vitamins, supplements or foods described in this book.

Each supplement is rated on the basis of factors like overall importance and cost-effectiveness are amalgamated into one nifty little number. Five dollar signs ($) being mandatory and should be included in your grocery list (if not, it's to your own detriment) and one dollar sign ($) being either not very good, too expensive and/or for very specific, special needs.

CHROMIUM - A trace mineral that crams glucose into muscles like an overzealous subway usher crams in people. Chromium is an insulin agonist, meaning the best time to take it is when eating a starchy, carbohydrate meal and insulin levels are elevated. This supplement also makes carb-loads more effective. Chelated form absorbs better.

RDA: 120 Micrograms

Sources: http://www.anyvitamins.com/chromium-info.htm ,
http://www.chromiuminformation.org/FOODS_ch romium_rich_foods.htm

Foods Rich in Chromium: Raw onions and tomatoes, romaine lettuce, grape juice

Rating: $$$$$

SOLUBLE FIBER - Adequate fiber supplementation can make a big difference in how much body fat you're moving, especially on a carb-restrictive diet like this one. Metamucil is your best bet. Take 5 -10 grams (one to two rounded teaspoons) a day, preferably after a meal. If you're not eating vegetables (i.e.: trying to establish ketosis), double that dosage. Insoluble fiber derived from whole grains, beans and varieties of bran are OK before a workout for some staying power and regular bowel movement, but eat sparingly when on the ketogenic diet.

RDA: 20-40 g of dietary fiber daily

Sources: http://www.dietary-fiber.info/ ,
http://www.wehealny.org/healthinfo/dietaryfiber/fibercontentchart.html

Foods Rich in Fiber: prunes, beans, figs

Rating: $$$$$

FLAXSEED OIL - A supremely important supplement

regardless of what diet you're on. Flaxseed oil is the premier source of healthy AHA Omega 3 fat, so take 2-3 tbsp a day minimum. I encourage you to take significantly more for better mental and physical health as well as glycogen storage. Liquid form has superior absorption to capsules, but it spoils quicker. Ignore the "consume within 8 weeks of opening" warning on the label... you maybe have half that time before it spoils (and you will know by its bitter taste).

RDA: None, but the National Institute of Health recommends four grams of Omega-3 fatty acids daily for adults, based on a 2,000 calorie diet.

Sources:
http://www.lifescript.com/channels/beauty/scienc e_of_beauty/finding_good_fats_in_your_diet.asp ,
http://ific.org/publications/factsheets/omega3fs.cf m

Foods Rich in Omega 3: flax, walnuts, herring, sardines

Rating: $$$$$

VITAMIN C - An antioxidant, an anti-catabolic agent to prevent muscle loss, and an overall swell vitamin. It converts fat to collagen, a critical component to healthy joints, so why not load up on 1000 mg of the stuff three times a day at these prescribed times: when you first wake up, before a workout and after a workout with your vitamin cocktail. If it's timed release, skip the dosage before your workout. Avoid having it after a high fat/low carb meal during ketosis establishment because it will convert some of the fat to collagen and possibly affect your macro nutrient ratios and likely cause mild stomach distress.

RDA: 60 mg daily

Sources:
http://lpi.oregonstate.edu/infocenter/vitamins/vita minC/,

http://www.naturalhub.com/natural_food_guide_f
ruit_vitamin_c.htm

<u>Foods Rich in Vitamin C:</u> oranges, grapefruit, strawberries

<u>Rating:</u> $$$$$

VITAMIN E - Promotes healthy heart, lungs and digestive
system, and can accelerate muscle repair. Take anywhere
from 200-1000 IU before an intense leg workout where
lasting soreness is anticipated and post workout. If you're
eating mayonnaise (gimme a sec... mmmm, mayonnaise.
Alright, I'm back), you can decrease your dosages, as this
delicious condiment is a good source of E.

<u>RDA:</u> 10 milligrams per day

<u>Sources:</u> http://www.hoptechno.com/book29b.htm,
http://healthlink.mcw.edu/article/983211401.html

<u>Foods Rich in Vitamin E:</u> nuts, vegetable oils, green leafy
vegetables, mayonnaise

<u>Rating:</u> $$$$$

ZMA - For those who don't know, this stands for Zinc
Magnesium and it's essential for healthy testosterone and
IGF-1 levels. For increased "T", use 30mg of zinc, 400-
500mg magnesium and 11 mg vitamin B6 and take before
bedtime on an empty stomach. If you're eating a lot of beef,
this suppliant won't be on the "A" list. Avoid using more
than 100mg zinc a day however, as this can increase the
risk of prostate cancer.

<u>RDA:</u> Approximately 400 mg.

<u>Sources:</u> www.trainwiser.com/90/684-zma-
testosterone-support.html,
http://www.clevelandclinic.org/heartcenter/pub/g
uide/prevention/nutrition/35powerfoods.htm

<u>Foods w/ Zinc, Magnesium and B6:</u> brown rice, spinach, kale, beets

<u>Rating:</u> $$$

DESICCATED LIVER TABLETS - A personal fave. Helps prevent muscle breakdown and creates red blood cells which will give you a righteous pump during your workout and help build muscle. Use it as a quick hit of protein and amino acids to keep everything humming along. Under the right conditions, it also promotes growth hormone release. I'll take anywhere from 3, 480 or 800 mg tablets after my beauty sleep and 10 or more on an empty stomach before a workout. Some "formulations" include citrus bioflavonoid 9a potent anti-oxidant), B12 and the enzyme bromelain (which assists in protein digestion), while others are straight-up dried-up liver in a pill. Both are good.

<u>RDA:</u> Unknown, so follow the manufacturers recommended dosage

<u>Sources:</u> <u>http://www.bodybuilding.com/fun/southfacts_liver.htm</u>, <u>http://www.healthcastle.com/iron.shtml</u>

<u>Foods w/ Equivalent Benefits:</u> liver, mussels, red meat

<u>Rating:</u> $$$$

POTASSIUM - Maintains fluids in muscle cells, which is critical for growth and fullness. It's a high priority supplement when on a fluid depleting diet, and it's cheap. They come in 99mg tablets (I'm not sure why), so take one to two tablets with every meal and snack and 2-6 tablets with your post-workout drink.

<u>RDA:</u> 3.5 grams daily

Sources:
http://www.pubquizhelp.34sp.com/sci/minerals.html, http://www.vaughns-1-pagers.com/food/potassium-foods.htm

Foods Rich in Potassium: bananas, melons, avocados, apricots

Rating: $$$$$

CARNITINE - Your body produces modest amounts of this essential nutrient, especially when you consume red meats on a fairly regular basis, but topping up supplies is what I'm suggesting if you want optimum fat loss. It works great with insulin-controlled diets like the Keto-Fu, and will help you feel more human when in the dredges of ketosis. I'd also tell you that it boosts the immune system and lowers cholesterol and triglyceride levels, but that'd be saying to much. Kind of pricey, but I encourage taking three grams with breakfast and another three before a workout IF your budget permits. If you can't, don't despair. Meats like liver, beef and beef heart are good sources and are foods that fit beautifully with the Keto-Fu.

P.S. You don't need to buy carnitine, just combine the amino acid L-Leucine and vitamin C. That makes carnitine! But don't sweat it anyway, the results are

mixed as to whether or not carnitine even works.

RDA: No RDA or Dietary Reference Intake (DRI) value has been established.

Source: http://www.lef.org/abstracts/codex/acetyl-l-carnitine_index.htm,
http://www.mynchen.demon.co.uk/Ketogenic_diet/Supplements/Carnitine.htm

Foods Rich in Carnitine: liver, beef, beef heart

Rating: $$$

NIACIN - AKA vitamin B3 promotes a healthy blood lipid profile as well as improved blood flow to muscle bellies for that awesome anabolic pump. Can reduce cholesterol. Take 100-200mg, optimally before resistance training.

RDA: 20 milligrams per day

Sources: http://www.hoptechno.com/book29i.htm, http://www.feinberg.northwestern.edu/nutrition/factsheets/vitamin-b3.html

Foods Rich in Niacin: beef liver, chicken, peanuts

Rating: $

CALCIUM - In addition to keeping bones and pearly whites healthy, it also reduces the risk of osteoporosis and cancer. Unless you're eating cheese, the Keto-Fu diet is rather restrictive when it comes to dairy consumption, ergo a possible calcium deficiency. Take 400-500mg a day, and

should be taken with a 1:1 or 1:2 ratio with magnesium.

RDA: 1000 milligrams per day.

Sources: http://ohioline.osu.edu/hyg-fact/5000/5557.html, http://www.vegansociety.com/html/food/nutrition/calcium.php

Foods Rich in Calcium: green leafy vegetables, dairy products, seeds nuts

IRON - I know, I know. You've heard horror stories about people with too much iron needing their blood drained (a vampire conspiracy, no doubt), but it's far overblown. Iron is essential in building blood and transporting oxygen via the blood superhighway, but if you're taking desiccated liver tablets on a daily basis, don't bother supplementing with it. However, if you're hardcore in the gym and packing on the slabs of meat, or if you take an iron-depleting e/c/a then you can safely supplement with 10mg during a meal.

RDA: 14 Milligrams

Sources:
http://www.pubquizhelp.34sp.com/sci/minerals.html,
http://www.eatwell.gov.uk/healthissues/irondeficiency/?view=textonly

Foods Rich in Iron: red meat, green leafy vegetables, lentils and beans

Rating: $

SELENIUM - This anti-oxidant makes other anti-oxidants like vitamin C and E more effective. Take 50mcg every time you take C and E (up to 200mcg) or 50-200mcd with post-workout vitamins.

RDA: 55 Micrograms

Sources:
http://www.pubquizhelp.34sp.com/sci/minerals.html, http://ods.od.nih.gov/factsheets/selenium.asp

Foods Rich in Selenium: brazil nuts, tuna, beef, cod

Rating: $$$

VANADIUM - This mineral works much like chromium (and you'll even see it "bundled" with some chromium supplements), however its soluble counterpart vanadyl sulfate absorbs much quicker and doesn't need insulin to work. Essential for bones and teeth. Take 25mcg daily, or double that dosage if you're using it as a glucose transporter.

RDA: There is no established RDA for vanadium.

Source:
http://www.healthvitaminsguide.com/minerals/vanadium.htm,
http://www.pdrhealth.com/drug_info/nmdrugprofiles/nutsupdrugs/van_0258.shtml

Foods Rich in Vanadium: mushrooms, shellfish, parsley

Rating: $$$

BREWERS YEAST - I tend to favor this glucose transporter over its brethren, chromium and vanadium, because it's cheaper and it has ample dosages of chromium anyway. Take 500-1000 (or even more won't hurt you, as I can personally attest) after a workout with a high-sugar creatine post-workout bevy.

RDA: Unknown, so follow manufacturers recommended dosage.

Sources:
http://www.vitaminuk.com/pages/articles/brewersyeast.htm,

http://www.findarticles.com/p/articles/mi_g2603/is_0002/ai_2603000229

<u>Foods w/ Equivallent Nutritional Properties</u>: lentils, kidney beans

<u>Rating:</u> $$$$

ACIDOPHILUS WITH BIFIDUS - It probably isn't very pretty down there to begin with, but on a ketogenic diet, fatty foods tend to loiter around the digestive system. Supplementing with Acidophilus ensures proper food assimilation and healthful bacterial balance, so taking three to five capsules a day with meals is a sound idea. Consult suggested usages for any deviations.

<u>RDA:</u> No RDA established

<u>Source:</u>
http://www.allstarhealth.com/lj_c/Acidophilus_Bifidus.htm,
http://findarticles.com/p/articles/mi_m3301/is_n7_v95/ai_15703031

<u>Foods Rich in Acidophilus and Bifidus Cultures:</u> yogurt

<u>Rating:</u> $$$

ENZYMES: LIPASE(FATS), PROTEASE(PROTEIN), BROMELAIN(PROTEIN), PAPAIN (PROTEIN) - Protein-based substances are a challenge for the digestive system, that's why the enzymes protease, bromelain and papain are the catalyst in the comprehensive assimilation and utilization of these amino acid packed foods. Lipase is different but equally important. It's the enzyme that converts lipids like cholesterol and triglycerides to free fatty acids and glycerol. Daily supplementation (under the direction of a physician) may be helpful while on the ketogenic diet.

RDA: Unknown, so follow manufacturers recommended dosage.

Sources:
http://science.howstuffworks.com/cell2.htm,
http://www.healingdaily.com/detoxification-diet/enzymes.htm

Foods Rich in Enzymes: raw fruits and vegetables

Rating: $$$

MULTI-VITAMIN – There are as many multi-vitamin formulas out there as hairs on Chewbacca's back, but don't be too perplexed trying to choose one. Buy one brand, and when that bottle is done, switch to another brand and another formulation. That way you're not getting a concentration of on particular vitamin or mineral. Better yet, take a break from multi-vitamins every other month for a week to prevent overdosing and to allow the body to cleanse itself.

Without any supplementation whatsoever, expect it to take 3 days or more before obtaining the holy grail of fat burning we now know as ketosis. Using repartition agents will hasten the process by a day or so, but coming off a 24 hour fast is best. Abstinence of food and water for a day should lower your blood sugar level to near ketosis state (circa 50 mg/dl if you're monitoring that sort of thing) and will shrink your appetite. You'll practically be catapulted into ketosis.

Yet something else you can do to speed the process is cardio. A big ole mess of it. Activities like running is a triple threat: it burns fat, whips up the metabolism and deplete glycogen stores in the muscles, so there's another reason to fire up the mp3 player and hit the pavement. It's early in the week too, so it won't be as grueling and utterly exhausting as when you're deep in ketosis country. Running in a state of ketosis causes an unholy burn in your legs and lungs, and wouldn't be considered fun unless you're a masochist.

Here's a trick a friend showed me which works well, provided you're doing some form of cardio. To force a state of ketosis, add whipping cream to hot herbal tea. Actually, my friend uses coffee, but according to the Canadian Diabetes Association: *"drinking caffeine in large amounts over a short period of time has been known to raise blood sugar. Caffeine does this by enhancing the effect of two hormones (adrenaline and glucagons). These two hormones release stored sugar from the liver resulting in high blood sugar."*

This means getting jacked up on caffeine before a run isn't going to give you the optimal fat burning effect you're looking for. Caffeine is also not a wise option for those with stress or anxiety disorders, so my advice is stay clear and opt for more natural sources of energy.

SUPPLEMENTATION PART DEUX: SUPER STACKS

Some vitamins compliment each other, like superhero's Batman and Robin, the JLA (Justice League of America) or even the hormonally-challenged Teen Titans.   Under the right situations, these dynamic combos synergize and create maximal benefits, and hopefully without intestinal discomfort (again, I am not a doctor – consult a professional health practitioner before taking any vitamins, supplements or foods described in this book).

JOINT PROTECTION

Flax oil 1-3 tsp

1100 mg. Cetyl Myristoleate

1500mg Glucosamine

400 mg Chondroitin (twice a day)

1000mg vitamin C

800 IU vitamin E

Note: I advise not taking this stack all at once, but rather staggering it with meals to avoid upset stomach.

BLOOD PUMP STACK

100-250mg Niacin

and/or 4-10 800mg desiccated liver tablets

and/or 5g arginine

EPHEDRA-FREE FAT BURNER

40-50mg capsaicin

90-100mg green tea tablets

500mg guggulsterones

1-2 650mg kelp (option)

LOW CARB / KETOGENIC

2g L-carnitine (ideal taken before cardio)

650mg kelp

4 800mg desiccated liver tablets

and/or 10g BCAA

Note: Take this whenever you feel depleted or hungry, up to 3 times daily and/or...

5-10g glutamine

20-60g whey protein

5g soluble fiber (i.e.: Metamucil)

CALORIE RESTRICTIVE / ANTI-CATABOLIC

5-10 glutamine

1000mg vitamin C

4 800mg desiccated liver tablets

and/or 10g BCAA

Note: Take this whenever you feel depleted or hungry, up to 3 times daily

NIGHT TIME

ZMA

5-10g glutamine

EFA's (Essential Fatty Acid aka flaxseed oil)

Note: Take on empty stomach

PRE-WORKOUT

5-10g glutamine

20g whey protein

or...

5g arginine

vitamin C

e/c/a (25mg ephedrine, 200mg caffeine, 80-325mg aspirin)

4 800mg desiccated liver tablets

and/or 10g BCAA

Note: Take this on an empty stomach

or...

5g arginine

4-10 800mg desiccated liver tablets

Note: This nifty combo is for getting a great pump during resistance training ;)

POST-WORKOUT

30-60g whey protein

40g *dextrose or maltodextrin

5g creatine

250mg alpha-lipoic acid

5g taurine (optional)

5g ribose (optional... very effective if you can find it!)

and...

1000mg vitamin C

800 IU vitamin E

10,000 IU beta carotene

Multivitamin

**500mcg chromium GTF (optional)

99mg potassium

*If you don't have dextrose or maltodextrin, don't sweat it. Use table sugar, Kool-aid, whatever.

**You can substitute chromium GTF with 800mg brewers yeast for similar effect.

SENSORY OVERLORD

THE CRISIS

The world will try and wear you down, fray your nerves, dull the senses bring the pain and steal your sleep like a thief in the night.

THE PLAN

Adversity can make the strong even stronger. In this chapter we'll sharpen the senses, increase your pain threshold and defeat stress and sleeplessness – to overcome and become Sensory Overlord!

FOUR WAYS TO SUPER VISION

I've got good news and bad news. The good news is, through a healthy diet and vision training, normal vision can be enhanced into super vision. Even poor vision and medical conditions like myopia, hypermetropia and astigmatism can be corrected either fully or in part (factors such as physical fitness and diet notwithstanding). But as I mentioned, there's also bad news. This "super vision" I speak of does not entail shooting laser-beams from your eyeballs or staring through peoples undergarments with x-ray vision. Sorry.

1. SUNLIGHT

There are two radically opposing viewpoints regarding exposure to sunlight and UV radiation. The more conventional viewpoint is that over-exposure to UV radiation without proper eyewear protection can lead to visual impairments ala retinal damage and cataracts. The less conventional school of thought supported by some highly-respected optometrists is that, in reality, directly staring into the sun improves eyesight and can assist the body in healing. Furthermore, they go on to say sunglasses that block the full spectrum of the sun and it's ultra violet rays deny the body precious alterative energy and is a contributing factor to the increasing number of people with eye disease and even blindness in North America. (Besides, dark sunglasses prompt the eyes to dilate and allow UV rays to enter anyway).

Perhaps it's not sunlight that we should shun, but rather the shiesty marketing propaganda from protective eyewear companies!

2.   DIET

Just as the brain is largely constituted of DHA omega 3 fatty acids, so are the cells of the eyes! With this knowledge in our *view*, we can plainly *see* supplementing with omega 3 is important as all heck. Fish like mackerel, sardines, Atlantic salmon (not the canned, fish-farmed stuff) and herring (my personal favourite) are excellent sources of DHA omega 3, but flaxseed and hempseed oil supplementation is also adequate and can be converted to DHA if taken in ample quantity. Other foodstuffs and supplements important in preventing Age related Macular Degeneration (AMD) and other vision robbing diseases are as follows:

Carotenoids Lutein and Zeaxanthin: Green vegetables (raw kale is a significant source of lutein), eggs and corn.

<u>Polyphenols Anthocyanins and Flavinoids:</u> Berries and their purplish plant pigmentation, gingko, biberry and eyebright.

Pantothenic Acid (a B vitamin), Nicotinamide adenine dinucleotide (otherwise known as NADH, a coenzyme made from vitamin B2, or niacin) and the antioxidant Acetyl-l-carnitine are also reputed to improve eyesight.

3. VISUAL SKILLZ

Being that 80% of all sensory input is visual, it would make sense to hone and amplify this most important perceptual power through which life is apprehended. Athletes and US Air force pilots know that to improve one's visual *skills* is to improve one's performance, just as poor visual skills correlates with poor performance. And studies prove it. Visual reaction time, eye/hand/body coordination, visual acuity and concentration (the ability to ignore extraneous visual stimuli otherwise known as "visual noise") all can be improved with practice. How? You may be surprised by the answer: video games. Research shows that playing action games one hour per day for 10 days can markedly improve important visual skills of non-gamers. However, not all games work, only those which demand attention to peripheral details and focus is distributed or switched from one area of a visual field to another (Medal of Honour was used in the study). Games where there is only one focal point at a time (in this case Tetris) had no improvement whatsoever of standard visual tests.

You Tube Title: **Video Games Can Improve Eyesight**

Tags: video   games   vision

From: dakotadunes44

4.   EYE EXERCISES

Here are a number of simple eye exercises, devised by William Bates, ophthalmologist, who first published his simple but effective vision therapy techniques in Better

Eyesight magazine way back in the 1920's. He later published a book called "The Bate's Method for Better Eyesight Without Glasses" which became the standard by which all other natural vision therapy books are measured. You can do these exercises practically anywhere and anytime, that will, over time, strengthen the eye muscles and improve conditions such as myopia, astigmatism, squints and lazy eyes.

- Palming – Close your eyes and cover them with the warm palms of your hands (you can warm them up by rubbing them together). Avoid exerting any pressure on your eyes. Relax and imagine staring into the blackest black. Do this for at least five minutes (30 minutes is recommended), three times a day.

- Swinging – Focus on a spot in the distance, and begin gently swinging your eyes from side to side. You can also rock your body from side to side, noting how objects within eyeshot move opposite to the direction you are swinging. Tip: keep a wide stance to avoid falling over!

- Tromboning – Hold up an object before your eyes at the full length of your arm. Now bring your arm in slowly until it touches your nose, all the while your vision should be locked in on the object. Now slowly move the object away from your face. Try breathing in as you bring the object closer, and breathe out as you move the object away.

- Clockwork – Facing a real or imaginary clock face straight-on, begin to look as far as you can directly up at the 12 o'clock position. Hold for two seconds and slowly return back to the center of the clock. Do this exercise for 60 seconds. There's more: look at 12 o'clock, hold for two seconds then move your eyes to the one o'clock position. Return back to 12 o'clock. Hold for two seconds and move to the two o'clock position. Repeat until you have gone all around the clock, then go counter-clockwise.

- Blinking – If your eyes feel dry and crusty, you can stimulate the tear ducts and induce tears by squeezing the eyes shut, then blinking quickly several times, then squeezing the eyes shut again. Or you can prepare a delicious onion casserole and weep your eyes better ;)

- Sunning – With closed eyes, look directly at the sun (or at an incandescent light bulb if you live in Siberia). Slowly rotate your head from side to side as you focus on the light. This may help peripheral vision as well as relax the eyeballs.

HEARING: QUIET IS THE NEW GOOD

Music has progressively gotten louder, heavier and more aggressive and recording technology has been progressing at an equal pace. It doesn't take an audiophile to notice how any given artists latest recording has gotten crisper, cleaner, punchier than their last release. But I'm hear to inform you the trend has changed, and blasting loud sonic music in your ears for extended periods of time is now passé. It's been done to death and it's killing our ears. It's destroying the hearing of our youth. There are 28 million cases of hearing loss in the United States alone, and over 35% of those cases are due, at least in measure, to exposure to detrimentally loud noises. Many of these cases are preventable and most of this type of hearing loss is permanent.

If you were listening in science class (or maybe you couldn't hear?) you'd know sound is a vibration of an object in motion, which causes air molecules to vibrate around it and arrange in patterns corresponding to the movement of the object. These patterns are transmitted *through and by* the air faster than torpedoes until they literally rattle your

eardrums. This vibration of the eardrum causes three tiny bones called ossicles to vibrate, which are then transmitted to the inner ear - and this is where critical and permanent damage to your hearing can occur. Vibrations set fluid within the inner ear (called the cochlea) swishing; thereby stimulating the delicate hair cells and nerves of the inner ear into code the brain can translate. A sledgehammer striking plywood can be discernibly heard from hundreds of feet away, yet many people listen to music at the same volume, from ear buds sticking directly in their ear! In this case, sound is less like a torpedo and more akin to an atomic bomb! Exposure to this kind of violent audio assault can and will cause what is called *sensori-neural hearing loss* (also known as *nerve deafness*) which is irreparable.

You Tube

Title: **TINNITUS- Can you hear that?**

Tags: tinnitus music fun sound rock hiphop rap ear hearing health movies ringing feature film girls guys

From: josecassella

EIGHT HEARING HACKS

Hacking hardware for better performance is fun, but hacking your sense of hearing for better performance and longer life is better. Here are some handy tips and tricks you can try to hear better, for longer.

1. Obtain people's attention before you speak, and be sure to give your full attention to others when they speak. This prevents people from yelling like the roof, the roof, the roof is on fire.

2. Exercise your hearing by trying to pick up conversations from selected distances. Try it in a busy room with a lot of background noise and see what you can make out. When you listen to music, zero your focus on a particular instrument. Take a walk down a quiet street, and really listen to all the sounds we are normally oblivious to. As you do these exercises again and again, you're ability to hear sounds around is bound to improve.

3. In noisy environments, pay attention to the body language of the one who is talking. Nobody likes to repeat themselves, but if they have to, they usually end up speaking even louder.

4. The ability to see words on a page doesn't do much good if you don't understand the language, and this analogy can be applied to hearing. You have to know what you're hearing. That's why it's important to be conscious of the little details in our life, what is often referred to as mindfulness. Pay attention to the little sounds around you, and what is making those sounds.

5. Studies from the University of California have

shown the right ear is better at deciphering the complex rhythms of speech, while the left ear is better at listening to musical tones.

6.   Clean your ears. I said, clean your ears! Q-tip's are okay for removing gobs of ear wax (a known cause of dizziness and nausea because it disrupts the functioning of the inner ear), but an ear syringe is better. Simply squirt warm water into your ears a few times while in the shower.

7.   For those with hearing aids, sit or stand so that noises are behind you and your facing, who you want to listen to. Electronic hearing apparatus work better when facing the sound.

8.   According to studies from the University of Tennessee in Knoxville, the nicotine patch was found to enhance the auditory/neural pathways of non-smokers, giving them the heightened ability to isolate and discern various background sounds. This in no way means that cigarette smoking improves one's hearing however, since cigarettes are loaded with other deadly and detrimental carcinogenic chemicals that can hurt one's hearing.

Here is a list of sounds, their decibel levels and the elicited human response for most normally-hearing adults:

SOUND/ACTIVITY	NOISE LEVEL (dB)	PHYSICAL RESPONSE
Threshold of hearing	0	Likely not audible.
Sound perception	10	Barely audible
Leaves rustling, soft jazz in the background, human whisper	20 - 30	Very quiet
Public library, kitchen/bathroom, computer, quiet office	40 - 50	Quiet
Normal conversation, commercial districts, light car traffic	55 - 60	Intrusive
Vacuum cleaner, loud conversation	65 - 70	Disruptive to telephone conversations
Busy traffic intersection, outboard motor, flashing red Bat-phone	75 - 80	Dang annoying
Passing motorcycle, busy city street, loud show, screaming child,	85 - 95	Can damage hearing after eight hours exposure per

lawnmower		day
Power saw, amplified rock music, squealing pigs, sandblaster, nightclub	102 110	Can damage hearing after a mere 30 minutes exposure per day
Amplified rock music (head-banging style), car horn, propeller aircraft, air raid siren, shotgun, hydraulic press	115 130	Threshold of pain. Can damage hearing after 3.7 minutes exposure a day
Jet engine, sonic scream of the Banshee™	140	Immediate danger
Blue whale	188	Immediate danger
Volcano	272	Hearing damage is the least of your worries

SOUND ADVICE

For those who love to rock out, let's acquaint our ears to lower volumes. Let's set limits to how loud we will listen to music, regardless of how good the song is. Studies establish that exposure to volumes of over 85 dB (decibels) for eight hours can damage your hearing, and it takes only four hours if the volume is 90 dB and above. Prevention is critical because this kind of hearing damage is not correctable. Rest your ears for a few days, and take a break from sounds altogether if it's possible. Wear earplugs or earmuffs if you have to (cotton jammed in the ear does <u>not</u> work because it's too porous). It's true what they say: silence is golden. It need not apologise to loud. Quiet is the new good.

HERBS FOR HEARING

Certainly, supplementing with health products is a distant second to prevention when it relates to hearing loss, but there have been some eyebrow raising, ear perking findings from the scientific world. For example Acetyl-L-Carnitine (ALC), a superior and more bioavailable form of the amino acid L-Carnitine, was shown to stave off age-related hearing loss in rats. The coenzyme Lipoic Acid faired well also in similar studies, with some rats even experiencing an improvement in auditory thresholds. Humans would be well to take upwards of 150 mg a day. Vitamins A and E, which you may have in the kitchen cupboard right now has similar positive effects, especially in preventing age-related hearing loss due to oxidization and the ravages of free radicals. Reports suggest daily dosages of 10, 000 IU a day for vitamin A and 400 – 800 IU for vitamin E.

CYBERNETICS... ON THE CHEAP

Disposable implants and Open-Source Prosthetics are here, and it seems we're more plugged in, dependent on, and integrated into technological devices and systems than we even care to admit. Even mankind's collective consciousness has been coded into ones and zeros, in a self-supporting binary ecosystem where we log into our online personas with avatar faces and interface with other digital representations of self. Man created technology, and in turn technology has recreated us. Meanwhile, robots become more humanoid by the day, and even reality itself has stiff competition from today's computer graphics imaging. Is this the Cybernetic Age? Has mankind been assimilated?

Time for a deep breath. Inhale in through the nose, exhale out the mouth. That's better. Even if humanity has reached version 2.0, it can't be all bad. Here are three cybernetic devices under $40 and five under $500 that suggests anyone - regardless of economic status or geography – can benefit from the advances of medical science.

1) FOR YOUR EYES ONLY - IMPLANTED INTRAOCULAR LENSES: This small-incision, sutureless surgery, developed by eye surgeon and philanthropist Sanduk Ruit, can be done quickly and outside a hospital, giving sight to the poor and blind for only $4

2) IT'S A GUT FEELING: ELECTRONIC SMARTPILL: Once swallowed, this vitamin-shaped wireless sensor radio's back information on the patient's stomach pressure and acidity and is dismissed out the bung hole several days later. The cost: $500

3) MUSIC TO YOUR EARS: SONGBIRD DISPOSABLE HEARING AIDS: No need for repairs or battery purchases, these disposable in-the-canal hearing aids come in one size, last 40 days and cost $40

4) REST ASSURED: SNORE GUARD DENTAL APPLIANCE: A small dental appliance, not unlike an athletic mouthpiece, can be worn at night and prevents the jaw and tongue from dropping back and obstructing the wind pipes. Only $27

5) WORD OF MOUTH PIECE: MINI DENTAL IMPLANTS: These non-invasive implants made of surgical-grade, bio-compatible titanium is quick

and easy to install and cost less than half the price of full-sized dental implant. Starting at $500

FOUR WAYS TO RELAX

1.   UNLOCK JAW, UNCLENCH FISTS

Go ahead; release the tension in your jaw. Doesn't that feel better? Keeping your jaw loosey-goosey during typically stressful situations may result in better performance and a more relaxed disposition. And you'll be less inclined to sucker punch somebody with those clenched fists of yours.

2.   THAT WAS HERE, THIS IS NOW

How can we make sound decisions and safely navigate our lives into the murky future ahead if we're not anchored in the present moment? Thinking can cause a lot of pain - and it's usually over something we have absolutely no control of - so it's better to free our mind of any preoccupations with the past or fears of the future and just live in the moment That's all we have control of anyway, is this very moment in time. The easiest way to achieve this mindfulness of the present is to do as the Buddhist monks do and follow your breathing. As soon as your mind wanders, gently bring it back and refocus on the current activity.

[The average person has 2000 to 3000 thoughts per day, while a high-level, focused athlete thinks less than a thousand thoughts (and they're all about endorsements). Buddhists have quieter minds still, and can hold an image in thought for up to 20 minutes. Most people cannot hold unto even a simple image for more than 10 seconds!]

You Tube

Title: **Never Mind the Noise**

Tags: work   corporate   life
meditation mindfulness buddhist love

From: LovingEvolution

3.   I SPY WITH MY LITTLE EYE...

Mind racing in fast forward? Here's a few ways to hit the slow mo: 1) Envision a loved one. Imagine giving them a warm hug and promise yourself you'll do so next time you see them in person again. 2) Play a favourite song, either in your head or sing it out loud (who cares if you sound like a screaming badger)? Some, like me, feel most at ease listening to hymns of faith, while others headbang to disco polka. Whatever yanks your crank. 3) Focus on a particular color in your surroundings. If you love the color purple, seek out something of that color and hone in on it with all your attention. A great way to unclutter the mind.

4.   DEEP BREATHS

Take a quiet moment and create some personal space for yourself. Take a deep breath in through the nose and slowly exhale through the mouth. Then, with your next breath, untighten all your muscles. Let it all hang out. Remember to breathe as before. Repeat as many times as needed.

SAMURAI IN TRAINING:

Philosophies of Buddhism and Zen mediation influenced the samurai culture to such an extent that some samurai gave up their violent lifestyle and became Buddhist monks.

SEVEN WAYS TO BE THE KING OF PAIN

A sprain, a broken bone, your mother-in-law. All can be a source of pain. But you can put pain in its place with these insights and strategies to increase your pain threshold, and you'll be able to achieve more and greater things!

1.   FITNESS LEVEL

The higher your fitness level, the higher your pain threshold. In fact, as you become more fit, the signals sent via the nervous system to indicate pain become muted. What was once a stabbing, rehabilitating pain to an unconditioned individual becomes a dull ache to the same individual after training and conditioning.

2.   CHEMICAL AND PSYCHOLOGICAL FACTORS

Underlying psychological/emotional problems like depression may be worsening your pain (or even the cause of it). In a study by Kurt Kroenke, a professor at the Indiana School of Medicine, more than half of depressed patients surveyed said they suffered from chronic pain, in the back, head, neck or stomach. Depression is a psychological state, but it's also chemical in the sense that retroactive peptides, serotonin and norepinephrine, regulate both mood and transmit pain signals. This means you're bound to get a two-for-one deal when you're already feeling down and out, and explains why 30% of people experiencing pain also suffer depression. If feelings of gloominess burden you and manifest in negative physical ways, you need to see your doctor. A doctor can (if he/she deems appropriate) prescribe medication for temporary relief and refer you to therapists for long term healing and resolution. On the other hand, if chronic pain is causing you to be depressed, don't overly emotionalise or personalise the experience.

[Finnish researches have found that those depression sufferers who had higher levels of vitamin B-12 in their blood responded better to anti-depressant medications than those with lower vitamin B-12 levels. B-1, B-2, B-6 and B Complex vitamins as well raise B-12 levels.]

3. POSITIVE ATTITUDE

Attitude is everything. Don't vex on what happens to you, but on *what you do with what happens to you*. Be committed to seeing the desired end results and you'll be better able to push through the pain. Here's a way of remembering how important a positive attitude is:

If every letter in the alphabet corresponded with a number: The letter "A" being the number one because it's the first letter, B would equal two, E would equal five and so on, what word and attribute would be 100% most important for

overcoming physical pain as well as the pains of life? It's not *manliness* or *power*, as I will show you:

$$M + A + N + L + I + N + E + S + S$$

$$13 + 1 + 14 + 9 + 14 + 5 + 19 + 19$$

$$= 92\%$$

$$P+O+W+E+R$$

$$16+15+23+5+18$$

$$=77\%$$

The magic word and 100% of dealing with pain and problems is *attitude*!

$$A+T+T+I+T+U+D+E$$

$$1+20+20+9+20+21+4+5$$

$$=100\%$$

Also keep in mind there is good pain and bad pain. Anesthesiologist Jay Yang, M.D., Ph.D., describes "good" pain as the kind that protects us and helps us survive. We burn our hand, we learn. "Bad pain," he says, "is pathological pain that persists long after your wound has healed. It serves no purpose." Bad pain may also be refered to as chronic neuropathic or "phantom" pain, which stems not from the originally damaged tissue but is rather a memory of pain that recurs over and over in the central nervous system. This is not to say chonic pain is not real - it is - but it's learned. The link between memory formation and chronic pain has been substantiated in at least one other study (albeit with mice). The smarter the mice, the more sensitive they were to pain.

4.   LACTIC ACID THRESHOLD

The arch-villain of cyclists, bodybuilders and Flash Gordon is what's known as the Onset of Blood Lactate Accumulation (OBLA). A build-up of lactic acid is ultimately what brings on that crazy burn (perceived as pain by the body) when running up a flight of stairs or repping out on weights, and said culprit is also largely responsible for the soreness felt days afterward. It's also believed the presence of lactic acid in muscle cells inhibits aerobic fat burning, so you can understand why improving our Lactic Threshold (LT) is so critical to progressing beyond our current physical limitations.

How is Lactate Acid produced? Lactate acid is a biochemical bi-product of energy consumption and movement. When we're engaged in intense physical activities ala weight training, sprinting for more than 10 seconds and stop starts sports like hockey, the body is forced to produces energy without ample amounts of oxygen. The key molecule responsible for the repositing and releasing of energy and the currency for most metabolic systems in the body is ATP (otherwise referred to as *adenosine triphosphate* by know-it-all personal trainers). ATP, and another important chemical compound called pyruvate (the ionized form of pyruvic acid) is gleaned from glucose and metabolized in cellular "power plants" called the mitochondria, where they're converted to energy with the help of oxygen. When the workload increases and oxygen becomes insufficient - as is typical of full contact chess and other high-intensity sports – the pyruvic acid converts to lactic acid and hydrogen ions. Lactate acid congregates in the blood, accumulating faster than the body can get rid of it (or be resynthesized into glucose in what's called the Cori Cycle), and the hydrogen ion concentrations create the acidity in the blood, throwing the bloods pH balance out of whack. Nerve endings are irritated and soon the nervous system as a whole is registering significant pain. Muscles become so jammed

with lactic acid they can no longer move. This when you've hit your lactic threshold, or Onset of Blood Lactate Accumulation (OBLA).

If we can delay the onset of lactic acid, we can train harder for longer, and better training equals better results. Let's explore methods to improve your lactate threshold.

5. OXIDATIVE ENERGY SYSTEMS

The most obvious strategy to increasing your lactate threshold is to improve the "oxidative energy systems" described above, so that your body utilizes oxygen more efficiently. At 70-80% of a trained athlete's maximum heart rate (MHR) and 50-60% in untrained athletes, these oxidative energy systems become oxygen deprived and lactic acid begins to accumulate. However, these numbers are in no way absolute, as there are a bazillion factors in play, and they aren't important because increasing your lactate threshold boils down to consistently training beyond your comfort level. Professional athletes who have plateaued and want to shave a half second off their best time need more detailed and systematic approaches, but for you and Bob down the street, training at a higher level of perceived effort will work. Bring on the lactate acid and the body will acclimatize in time. It will learn to buffer the lactic acid concentration in the bloodstream so the Onset of Blood Lactate Accumulation (OBLA) doesn't stop you in your tracks.

6. MAKE MORE MITOCHONDRIA

If you suspect your lactate threshold is lower than another person of the same physical conditioning, it could be an insufficient amount of mitochondria in your muscle cells. Similarly, fast twitch Type IIb muscle fibres - the muscles used for sprinting and powerlifting – accumulate lactic acid quickly because they've inherently less mitochondria and myoglobin and aren't nearly as efficient at utilizing oxygen. Even so, there's evidence you can change muscle fibre

types. The bodybuilders favourite Type IIb muscle fibres (that specialize in hypertrophy and are white in appearance) can be converted to a long distance runner's Type I muscle fibre (which are rich in blood and red). How? With a lot of endurance training. It works the other way too. By employing explosive movements and tempo changes in a regular training program - say for example sprinting or fartleks - you can make the quad muscles as hypertrophic as heck. Ever look at Olympic sprinters legs?!

7.   SODIUM BICARBONATE BUFFERING

Use prescription drugs or cellular trickery to delay the onset of blood lactate accumulation? Naw! A club soda might be all you need to keep the lactic acid burn at bay. It's because of the sodium bicarbonate inside, which acts as an alkalizing agent and reduces acidity in the blood. Try drinking a can a half hour before training legs and see if it works for you.

POLEMICS OF PAIN

Despite conventional wisdom which states women, due to the demands of child birth labour, are better at tolerating pain, studies are showing it's actually men who have the higher pain threshold. Men can thank a protein called GIRK2 which not only helps mitigate pain, but gives men a better and more effective response to painkillers.

Red-heads feel more pain. Literally. This is due to a dysfunctional melanocortin 1 receptor found in people with red hair.

An enzyme used in the metabolisation of the neurotransmitter dopamine, called catechol-O-methyl tranferase (COMT), can largely determine whether we have superhuman abilities to endure pain or not. This is due to wo forms of COMT, the weaker form produces methionine which is less effective at clearing dopamine, while the second form produces the more effective valine. Ergo, those imbued with valine feel less pain.

Photo by darkpatator / Fred

QUICK TEST O' THE NERVES

Having nerves of steel are cool, but nerve endings should be able to discern different sensations too. Here's how you can find out if that's the case: Have the individual close his or her eyes, and touch the skin of their arms and legs with a q-tip or a toothpick. They should be able to tell you whether it was soft or pointy. If not, see a doctor.

MAMA NSAID NO: SIX NATURAL PAINKILLERS

Your body can anesthetise itself if only given the chance. How often do we run to the medicine cabinet at the first hint of pain? But are we ultimately doing our bodies more harm than good? Over-reliance to painkillers mutes the bodies own anesthetisation capabilities, and a US government advisory panel, formally known as the Non-prescription Drug Advisory Committee, warned that overuse and overdosaging of analgesics and non-steroidal anti-inflammatory drugs (NSAIDs) can cause internal bleeding and kidney damage. Over-the-counter products containing one of more of said medicinal ingredients include: aspirin (Anacin, Bufferin), acetaminophen (Tylenol), ibuprofen (Advil, Motrin) and naproxen (Aleve) and this list is by no means exhaustive.

So what is the biochemical's responsible for anesthetisation, and how can we stimulate their production when we need it? Neurotransmitters serotonin and norepinephrine (the latter is also a hormone released from the adrenal glands) regulate both mood and transmit pain to the brain. Endorphins are also a naturally-produce pain-killers, relied on by athletes when they push their limits, and we can't forget the neurotransmitter and hormone adrenaline (relied on by thrill seekers and crooks running away with your television). The ways of coaxing their analgesic powers are as thus:

1. FOODS

Chocolate can evoke psychopharmacologic and chemosensory effects like few other foods. For one thing, chocolate sports biologically active constituents (methylxanthines, biogenic amines, and cannabinoid-like fatty acids), which incite psychological sensations similar to other addictive substances. When chronic pain has got you down, instead of popping pills, try eating a Hershey chocolate bar. Chocolate stimulates serotonin and dopamine levels which bring pleasurable psychological sensations. Chilli peppers can also turn up the good and turn down the suck with a release of endorphins. The hotter the pepper (Tepín, Habanero and Savina peppers being the hottest) the bigger the "endorphin dump". Just be sure to handle with care.

2. MEDITATION

Insight meditation is so desperately needed in this culture of want, suffering and distraction. Eric Lander, the director at the Whitehead Institute Center for Genome Research, MIT, prefigured that maybe in 10 years there will be a Surgeon General's recommendation for meditation and other such mental training mental exercises five times a week. Meditation can stimulate endorphin production in the body and help you feel peaceful and revitalised.

3. LAUGH IT UP

Research shows laughing can boost the immune system and is analgesic in nature because it releases endorphins in the brain and suppresses the production of stress hormones. It's good for the central nervous system and endocrine system and will help improve your mood and attitude, dude.

4. GET THE POINT

There's a growing body of evidence that acupuncture needles into specific body points will trigger the production of endorphins, as well as UV exposure from sun tanning beds which offer pain relief and feelings of elation (which would explain it's addictiveness for some).

5. TRANSFERENCE

If it's in a physically competitive setting (be it cycling, running, boxing) and you're feeling an intense lactic acid burn, fatigue or some other form of acceptable, non life threatening pain, it's better to refocus on your performance and not your pain. Try mico-managing your mechanics so your form is tighter (pain and exhaustion have a way of making people sloppy) and concentrate on your strategy. Also, make your opponent aware of their pain, and push them harder when you see them flinch. Make them hurt so bad they quit.

SPETSNAZ IN TRAINING:

Spetsnaz is a general term for "special-purpose forces" (divisions include Naval, Army, Ministry of Interior and counter-terrorist/anti-sabotage units). Trainees are armed with only a spade is shut in a room without windows along with a mad attack dog. Either the soldier learns to defend himself, or he becomes dog food!

6. MUSIC

Studies at McGill University demonstrated music delivers a mighty neurological impression and engages the very same neural clusters that process the rapturous responses to chocolate, sex and even street drugs. Music gets the brain neuron firing on all fronts: areas that process musical pitch, rhythm, melody and harmony, the cerebral throne of emotion and even short and long term memory all light up like a Christmas tree. In fact, electro chemical activity, cranial blood flow, heart rate, respiration and skin temperature all tend to spike when the listener hears a favourite song! Like Bob Marley says in the song "Trenchtown Rock":

One good thing about music / Well, it helps you feel no pain / So hit me with music; / Hit me with music now.

10 WAYS TO SUCCUMB TO THE SANDMAN

Sleeping disorders are the third most common patient complaint, surpassed only by headaches and the common cold. Approximately 15% of the adult population in the United States has insomnia severe enough to seek medical attention while fifty million Americans occasionally use some form of sleep medication. With those kinds of staggering numbers, it seems that figure of folklore, the mythical Sandman, is sleeping on the job. Take matters in your own hands. Here are 10 tips on ensuring you get the zees you need to take on the world.

1) Avoid bright lights, make room dark by using black garbage bags on windows

2) Don't do any exercise or heavy thinking an hour before bed.

3) Eating carbohydrates before bed may help you relax, but you'll be a deeper sleeper if you drink a glass of water with dissolved glutamine on an empty stomach. If you simply must eat before bed (guilty as charged), choose foods rich in the sleep-inducing amino acid tryptophan, such as turkey and other poultry, soy and dairy products, natural peanut butter and sunflower seeds.

4) Along with boosting anabolic hormone levels, ZMA may boost your chance of getting quality sleep too. The blend is 30mg zinc, 450mg magnesium and 11mg vitamin B6, but use sparingly unless you resistance train at least 3 times a week.

5) Do you toss and turn at night and wake up feeling as if someone worked you over with a baseball bat? It could be an old, worn mattress that's causing you sleep problems, and if so, look into getting a new one. As well, don't use bed for anything but sleep and - winks twice, grins, nudges playfully with elbow - procreational purposes.

6) If you want to sleep better, don't use medications to induce sleep or wakefulness. Allow your body to naturally regulate itself. Anyone dependent on medications/stimulants/depressants (which include caffeine and alcohol) should take the earliest possible opportunity (a vacation or even a weekend) to abstain completely and re-establish healthy sleeping habits. However, if you feel you must drink coffee or other caffeinated beverages, restrict them to the early part of the day. Any substance that, when withdrawn from, gives you headaches, the sweats and severe drowsiness can be classified as "toxic" to the body. Likewise, caffeine is habit-forming, intensifies feelings of anxiety, irritability as well as produce insomnia.

7) Lower the temperature of room the room and crack open a window. Cold and fresh air will be beauty for your sleep.

8) If at all possible (swing and continental shifters move on to the next pointer) wake up same time everyday. Try to keep a strict routine.

9) Because of a tightly integrated mind-muscle connection with the muscles of speech (when you even think of talking, our sub vocal speech muscles become alert and tense), you need to a) relax the muscles associated with speech: tongue, lips, jaws and cheeks and b) don't even think of saying anything.

10) Pray and read the scriptures. Jesus Christ is the Author of Peace, and true peace can only come through Him, so pray and ask for it. Likewise, reading the Bible and other holy scripture can bring calm and peace like no other literature.

DOMINO EFFECT OF SLEEP DEPRIVATION

The first crashing domino of adipose tissue is the increased appetite that's triggered when sleep deprived, no thanks to

a drop in leptin (the feel-full hormone) and the rise of the ghrelin (the "feed-me" hormone). Now you're tired, hungry and energy is in low supply, so you opt for a sugar rush and your sleep-weakened metabolism can't cope. Soon, the sugar high becomes a free fall, your bodies made a deposit in the fat bank, and you're more tired than ever! Ensure you get adequate sleep and you'll prevent negative hormonal activity and bad judgement from ruining your health.

TIRED BUT WIRED: HOW TO FUNCTION WITHOUT SLEEP

Another cause of looking bloated or the lack of fat loss could be insufficient sleep. It's proven: a lack of sleep will frustrate fat loss. Studies show those who sleep less tend to be overweight, due to two crucial hormones - ghrelin and leptin - that regulate our appetite. Those who habitually sleep less than 7-8 hours a night have 15% more of ghrelin, the hormone that makes us feel hungry and 15% less leptin which acts to suppress appetite. Getting ample sleep will make maintaining or losing weight easier. It's another example of how hormones (and how effectively we moderate them) profoundly affects our well-being.

But if you have an anxiety or sleeping disorder or even switch shifts at work, here are some strategies for getting through the day: First of all, eat extra healthy when sleep deprived. Fruits will give you a boost of vitamins and energy, and eating lots of vegetables will give you staying power. Load up on the vitamins (a multi, C and E at minimum), take 5-10 grams of glutamine twice a day and keep your diet clean, meaning free of saturated fats, high-glycemic carbohydrates and sugar. In short, eat light.

Economize your movements. You'll notice endurance runners economize their movements during a marathon, to conserve energy. Your marathon is the long day ahead of you. Find the shortcuts to any strenuous activities. Think like a slacker and look for the easy way, or ask someone to help you. Keep physical activities to a bare minimum, and if you absolutely must work out (an obsessive compulsive thing), keep it light. Stay stress-free. Allowing yourself to get angry, frustrated or overly-depressed will only

compound your energy-deficit problems and make the experience nightmarish. Instead, look at it another way. You now have extra time for yourself. Watch a movie, read a book or write a poem for someone you love. Get stuff done. Maybe it's time to get that truckload of laundry out of the way, or scrub down the bathroom. It's unlikely you feel like going out and "having fun" anyway, so why not get the odious chores done? That way, when you do finally sleep better, you can devote your time to things you want to do. Do something nice for someone. This has obvious benefits. You will feel better for having done something nice, the beneficiary feels better about themselves and about you, and it changes what could be a negative experience into a positive one. Finally, be comforted in the fact work performance won't suffer significantly when sleep deprived. Even if you've have a horrible week (or even *month*) of poor sleep, know it won't have a catastrophic effect. You may even surprise yourself on how productive you are on the job. And if you have kept in good shape, you're still probably more effective than the general population of couch potatoes.

GREEN BERETS IN TRAINING:

Food and sleep deprivation are used in training to condition commandos for possible capture by the enemy. Trainees typically lose 15 lbs after such conditioning exercises.

EASE ANXIETY DISORDERS

Lower insulin levels have a calming effect, and the brain responds well to high fat diets, in particular Omega 3, something your brain is partly composed of. If you are prone to high anxiety or stress, depression or neurological disorders like OCD and Bi-Polar, a low-carb, high EFA diet

will help stabilize your moods. The ketogenic diet was actually designed to treat children with pediatric epilepsy (way back in 1921 by a Dr.Wilder FYI) and was successful where other medications and treatments failed.

There's also Kava Kava (aka Piper methysticum), a natural root extract used to relieve anxiety and promote relaxation. The active ingredient in Kava Kava are phytochemicals called kava lactones and what's believed to treat depression and anxiety, so look for at least 30% kava lactones for maximum potency. Taking 100-200 mg of standardized extract three times a day should improve your emotional state, but because it depresses the nervous system, don't consume with alcohol or other anti-depression medications. Under rare circumstances where large dosages are taken over long periods of time, Kava Kava may cause liver disease.

SPEED OF ENLIGHTENING

THE CRISIS

We're bombarded with sub-conscious suggestions, unknowingly manipulated and dumbed-down by big media, and pacified by The Man! Wake up, it's time for your sleeping pill!

THE PLAN

Unlock the majestic potential of your mind with these awesome hacks and control your destiny, instead of somebody controlling it for you!

LEARN THE LOVE STARE

Disclaimer: This information is for entertainment purposes only. Don't be a creep. Only use this psychological tactic on consenting individuals!

A heroic act, a moonlight walk, a heartfelt poem hand written on parched paper; these are a few of the ways of capturing someone's heart. But there's another method, which cannot be purchased and requires no premeditated thought, and it can make a person of the opposite gender fall hopelessly and deeply in love with you within two minutes. It's called the Love Stare.

It's easy. First, you need to be face-to-face with your subject; the one you wish to fall in love with you. As you engage in polite banter, repeatedly lock eyes with the person. Researchers from Dartmouth College, University of Bristol and the University of Aberdeen concluded in the Sept. 2002 Psychological Science journal that mutual eye contact is a powerful indicator of positive human interaction, and by gazing directly into his or her eyes, you are attributing to this other person a strong message of romantic attraction. You may only need of a few seconds of this powerful nonverbal communication for the effect to take hold. Now, naturally disengage from the conversation and continue on as if nothing happened.

But something did happen between you two. There will be a change in the other person from that point forward, as there will likely be a change you. The person will think differently of you. The person will be in love with you!

THREE POWERFUL TACTICS OF PERSUASION AND MANIPULATION

"Without knowing the force of words, it is impossible to know men." -- CONFUCIUS

Words can be a devastating weapon, a healing salve or a tool of manipulation and coercion. Discover the methods top business negotiators, "compliance professionals" and savvy marketers use to get what they want.

Compliance is an important word here, because many if not all of us subconsciously engage in automatic, autogenic compliance to cope with the ever increasing volume of subliminal and perceived external messages. We have what social psychologist Robert Cialdini dubs an automatic response to "fixed-action patterns", which in layman's terms means we make snap decisions as a decision making short cut to save us time and mental energy on what we perceive are routine and innocent requests and statements. Unfortunately, these vanilla, automated trigger responses leave openings ripe for exploitation, and these exploits are used on us all the time.

I'll explain what this all means, and I'll start with an age-old and ubiquitous persuasion technique used by all cultures around the world. It's called:

THE RULE OF RECIPROCATION

Ever been given a free sample in a grocery store or in the mail and ended up buying the product, even when it might have been more expensive than a competing brand? Have you ever felt grateful and indebted to someone because they proffered you a gift or a favour? If you haven't, feel free to stop reading and return to the planet from whence you came. For the rest of us who can relate, we have unwittingly participated in the powerful socialization principle known as the rule of reciprocation or "The Golden Rule". It's an esteemed as THE Golden rule because it's based on the moral principle "treat others as you would like to be treated" and it's a crucial element in the evolution of human civilization. It's the precept endorsed by all societies and major religions, and our understanding and compliance to this Golden rule is embedded in our brains from an early age. Non-compliance inherently brings shame and alienation.

When one sees the full breadth of the rule of reciprocation, it is easy to see why the offering of favours and small gifts can cause the intended recipient to feel the heavy psychological burden of obligation to return the kindness, often when the gift or favour was not even accepted. The burden of debt can be so significant, people usually respond by returning more than they received, just to ensure they are no longer owe anything and are perceived as good-natured and in good standing.

The rule of reciprocation can be an effective negotiation tool, but it should be only used in good faith and to forge a win-win agreement.

GET THE HONEST GOODS

 David J. Lieberman PhD, in his book "Get Anyone to Do Anything and Never Feel Powerless Again", describes how one can coax out someone's true opinion of something. It works by being casual when asking for an opinion, and not by badgering (which induces the opposite effect). It's a simple follow-up question, which gives the person being asked more range to be honest and forthright. Here's how it goes: when you ask a friend for their opinion on a class presentation you've just made, you're likely to get a favourable homogenous response, something like "yeah, it was great. I found it quite interesting". That kind of response is meant to be encouraging, but it gives you no real information. You might as well have asked a tree. With common and useless like this, follow up with the question: "How could I have made the presentation more engaging?" The reason a follow-up question like this works, says Lieberman, is because you're admitting your presentation wasn't perfect, and honesty usually precipitates more honesty.

TALK THE "TOP OF THE LINE"

Cheesy late night television infomercials use this bartering trick a lot. After describing their product, they give what they feel is the estimated value of the product, at what they supposedly could charge at retail. This price is typically outlandishly high - and they know it - so they then introduce what is called a "limited time offer" at a lower price. To the viewer watching at home at 3 a.m., the latter price looks fair, especially in contrast with the first price. The comparison can hardly be helped and often the purchase is made, even when in reality the price wasn't all that hot.

In business and labour strike negotiations, it's often called the rejection-then-retreat technique. The first offer is unreasonable and rejected, as is anticipated, but the proceeding offers are often accepted, and with a higher level of satisfaction to the one in agreement. Why the high level of satisfaction? Because the recipient feels (rightly or wrongly) that they participated in the negotiation process and earned the deal.

Conclusion: These methods of coercion can be very effective, and for this reason should be used only with scrupulous intentions. It's important to be aware of them, and to be more conscious and deliberate in our thinking and decision-making processes.

ONE IMPORTANT RULE ABOUT STUDYING

The easiest, best way to learn is when you're interested in the subject matter. Quite simply, the more engrossed you are in the studying, the more your mind will drink up details and grasp concepts. You internalize and personalize the information, thereby owning it. The subject becomes almost second nature.

However the trick isn't the best way to learn, because we already know that.

The challenge is, how can we become interested in a subject we find as dull as directions on a shampoo bottle? Answer: find a study place more boring than the subject matter itself. This may be difficult, as I can personally attest, but it can be done. I've resorted to studying while waiting for a bus, and while on the bus of a quiet and familiar route. I've read and pondered under a big cottonwood tree in the middle of a grassy field. I've applied mnemonic tricks in the doctor's office. I use the empty spaces of time that are completely useless otherwise.

When you isolate yourself to a place and situation that deprives your mind of stimulation, that textbook on differential geometry begins to look pretty darn sexy.

THREE INGREDIENTS FOR A SHARP MIND

1.   CRAM FOR CARBS

Anyone involved with tasks demanding quick, intense cognitive processing will do well to eat a carbohydrate-rich meal. Reason being, your brain uses glucose for energy like a politician uses empty promises, so eat fruit or multi grain bread 20-30 minutes before pick up hockey or calculating your income taxes is a wise idea.

2.   CREATINE BUILDS MENTAL POWER

Studies suggest the ultra-popular amino acid supplement creatine used to increase muscle size and strength creatine helps users fare better at memory and time-restricted problem solving. In a completely different study, creatine was shown to protect the brain from head injury, Lab rats had been subjected to head injuries akin to human concussions, and the longer the rat had been taking creatine, the less brain damage the rat sustained.

3. GLUTAMINE

Glutamine is brain food. It serves as a substrate for the production of glutamate, the most common neurotransmitter to the brain, and gamma-aminobutyric acid, which is generally referred to as GABA. Glutamine also supports the nervous system with energy when glucose stocks get scarce. Ergo, glutamine can give you energy and brighten your mood when low-carbing it.

You Tube

Title: **Memorization Course**

Tags: jediairmech   memorization memory   lesson numbers   letters

From: Jediairmech

BUILD A SUPER-FAST BRAIN – THE MEGA LIST

You love to get your tweak on when it comes to optimizing and overclocking your computer, so why wouldn't you want optimal performance out of your brain? Here's what you need to know to increase your intelligence, both in the short and long term. It's all the best tips, tricks, tweaks and secrets for boosting brainpower, all in one place. No cruft, only the good stuff.

1. Something on the tip of your tongue, and your memory? Get the two hemispheres of your brain talking to each other by shifting your eyes horizontally for 30 seconds. Another way of jarring the memory is by speaking like-minded words out loud, one word after the other, until the word or thought is coaxed out.

---

2. Whether it's the steam increasing blood flow to the brain, or the restoring powers of negative ions, a hot shower has a way of firing the frontal lobe on all cylinders. Try it the next time you get a mental block.

3. Studies from University of Massachusetts Lowell (UML) suggest apple juice can actually "juice" production of the essential neurotransmitter acetylcholine as effectively as some medications, thereby goosing memory. Another fantastic fruit is blueberries, which might be the best anti-oxidant fruit you could eat to prevent toxic free radicals from ravaging your brain like a street thug.

4. Study after study concludes physical exercise benefits the brain. In fact, the odds of mental deterioration decrease by 13% with every mile a woman walks, says one study.

5. Proceedings of the National Academy of Sciences published the findings of UCLA psychologists who state multi-tasking impedes learning. However, this should not be confused with "hybrid activities", which consist of mental engagement plus physical movement in a social environment. Hybrid activities may include learning a new sport, coaching or dancing.

6. One study showed socially interactive people have a 42% less chance of dementia, so get out there and make friends and influence people.

7. Avoid garlic. Studies are showing the sulphone hydroxyl ions act as a toxin to human brain cells and desynchronizes brain waves, much in the same way it is harmful to dogs. Those suffering from headaches and Attention Deficit Disorder (ADD) might also benefit from holding off on garlic in all forms.

8. Television is the enemy of intelligence. Television appeals to the lowest common denominator with the most cost-effective formulaic programming. Only a handful of transnational media conglomerates own the media in United States now, and they control the flow of information. Television is a medium they use to distract you from the real issues by relentlessly pushing products they own down your throat.

9. Most older people blame their brains for poor memory, when the culprit is actually the weakening ability to filter out distraction, states the findings of UC Berkeley neurologists. So if your memory sucks, maybe you need to find quieter surroundings.

10. Sleep is crucial for good memory and concentration, and lead researcher Jan Born, from the Department of Neuroendocrinology at the University of Luebeck in Germany says it can be improved further by about 8% by applying an electric current at a particular frequency during non-rapid-eye-movement (non-REM) sleep.

11. Caloric-restrictive diets reverse aging of the mind and body by preventing cellular death, and numerous studies on animals have shown it extends life significantly.

12. Improve mental capacities by a) lowering your blood pressure through vigorous exercise, healthy eating, and eschewing alcohol, b) raising your good HDL cholesterol by avoiding refined carbohydrates, ditching trans fats and exercising your big booty, and c) lowering homocysteine levels by adding vitamins B6 and B12 your diet.

13. According to a May 2006 article in Neuron, the prospect of future reward enhances one's learning and memory capabilities. If there is an incentive for you to learn, you will learn it quicker. Fear is a

contra-incentive, but it tends to be an equally effective motivational tool.

14. Learn a new language. Bilingual people typically have better focus and longer attention spans than monolingual folk. And no, ebonics doesn't count.

15. Meditation, as used by Buddhist Monks, shows to improve neuroplasticity of the brain (the ability of the brain to physically change in response to stimulus and activity and believed to be the physical mechanism of learning). Insight meditation also allows one to interface with the here and now, and make clearer, more realistic decisions based on the present, and not clouded by the past or future.

16. Merely 10 one hour sessions of mental exertion and stimulation can have lasting and profoundly

17. positive affect on your thinking, so apply your mental facilities to the New York Times word puzzle and get your brain buff.

18. A six year study demonstrated eating two servings a day of dark green, leafy vegetables rich in folate and vitamin C will make you mentally sharper than the cheetos-eating dude who jutted his stained orange finger at you and laughed, saying you eat too much rabbit food.

19. Glutamic acid, when ingested in whole, unprocessed proteins like soy and shellfish, is a quick way to fire up the neurons and temporarily increase mental capacities. However, in the processed state of monosodium glutamate (MSG), it is a known neurotoxin and harmful to the body and brain. To get your glutamic acid fix before the big test, opt for whole natural foods from this gargantuan list 999 Foods Highest in Glutamic acid which is based on levels per 200 calories.

20. Stop "selfing". Introspection is good, up to a point, but when it becomes narcissism, selfishness or paranoia, studies show it affects your ability to concentrate on important tasks that demand full sensory involvement. Maybe all you need to do to boost your mental capacities is get over yourself.

21. Herbal supplements like lemon balm, ginkgo biloba and folate are reputed to quicken the mind, boost memory and stave off depression, respectively speaking. Amino acids like L-carnitine and L-Glutamine are also critical to optimal mental health, and even creatine (the bodybuilder's favorite supplement) is flexing its benefits for the brain in a number of recent studies.

22. When Elizabeth Barrett Browning penned the timeless phrase "How do I love thee? Let me count the ways...", she might've been talking about chocolate, in which case their are at least two. The first is how chocolate causes the brain to produce natural opiates which makes you feel marvy. The

23. second is the theobromine / phenylethylamine duo of awesomeness, which helps you feel alert and smart as all heck.

24. Acculturation is key. Expose yourself to new cultures, new systems and new ways of thinking. Does this mean you need to vacation in China or move to Africa? No. It may be a simple as going to your local small business magazine retailer and exploring the many different magazines with it's diversity of subcultures. Read. Immerse yourself in their universe.

25. Read the popular science and technology-related news website Slashdot.org everyday. It offers a diverse range of topics with intelligent discussion from some pretty smart people. And no, I'm not a paid shill for The Man, but I've been a reader for nearly 10 years and it's broadened my mind.

26. Unplug from the matrix. Push away from the computer desk, switch off the cell and the pager, and disconnect from cable television forever. Use a microwave? Throw it out. Is your digital alarm clock close to your head when you sleep at night? Push it way. The electromagnetic radiation emitting from digital-electronic devices shrinks brain cells and causes rapid cellular aging. The other reason for unplugging from the matrix is because it will allow you to think clearly and reassess your life without distraction.

27. Think "outside of the box". You can acquire this skill by avoiding common sources of information and questioning what you do think you know. Allow those you consider to be proficient out of the box thinkers to mentor you, preferably a variety of people with radically different skill sets. Get outside your comfort zone. Embrace novelty and new experiences. Invite the unknown and consider the impossible, as it may be impossible only within

28. the parameters of your own understanding and yet a reality to others.

29. Drinking alcohol kills brain cells, and it has the nasty habit of making people look like red-faced, loud mouthed fools. It also has the unenviable reputation of causing dementia in the brain. Tobacco doubles the risk of dementia, so abstain and be sane in the membrane.

SECRETS OF "THE SECRET": SIX LAW OF ATTRACTION HACKS

"The Secret" works, if you know how to use it effectively. First, for those few on the planet who have not heard what the secret is, let me explain. "The Secret" is a hot-selling book and a clever repackaging of The Law of Attraction, the age old principal that Buddha summed up best: "All that we are is the result of what we have thought." This means that the thoughts that predominantly occupy your mind ultimately become your reality, even if you don't want them to.

But it goes further than that. The Law of Attraction presupposes, and science now supports, that thoughts are energy, a signal if you will, that is transmitted out into the universe. And because everything in the universe is intimately interconnected (in ways not readily apparent to human understanding), your thoughts are received by the people and things you thought about. How accurate is the connection rate? 100% of the time. The universe never, ever gets it wrong. Ever had an instance where you were thinking about someone in your past, and then all the sudden they surface out of nowhere? Of course you have. That's The Law of Attraction in Action. Here are six hacks to making "The Secret" work for you:

1. *"All matter originates and exists only by virtue of a force... We must assume behind this force the existence of a conscious and intelligent Mind. This Mind is the matrix of all matter."* - Max Planck (Nobel Prize in Physics 1918). If you want someone to come (back) into your life, think about them oft. Your thoughts will be picked up by the person (albeit subconsciously). How long before they reciprocate consciously depends on a number of factors, like how many signals they are receiving, how much "noise" is in their life, how busy they are etc. It may be a single thought that get's them showing up on your Facebook, or it could be months, even years.

2. *"Imagination is everything. It is the preview of life's coming attractions."* - Albert Einstein 1879-1955. You need to be specific with your thoughts, which is why visualization is key. Engage all the senses if you can, to make it more real. Athletes use

visualization techniques all the time with great success (it's as important as the physical training itself, if not more so). If you ask for generalities, you get generalities.

3. *"What you resist persists."* - Carl Jung 1875-1961 Be positive when using the Law of Attraction. You can use thought energy to repel something or someone away from your life (with great effect, trust me on this one) but the person, place or thing will still be in your mind. No good. A better way is to focus only on what you want.

4. *"Ineffective people live day after day with unused potential. They experience synergy only in small, peripheral ways in their lives. But creative experiences can be produced regularly, consistently, almost daily in people's lives. It requires enormous personal security and openness and a spirit of adventure."* – Stephen R. Covey. Work with it. Use your strengths. The Law of Attraction works better, faster, if there is a synergy. Possessing the corresponding skill set to your want will facilitate your visualization becoming a reality.

5. *"But be ye doers of the word, and not hearers only, deceiving your own selves."* -James 1:22 The object of your desire will not drop out of the sky and onto your lap. The Law of Attraction doesn't work that way, and The Secret nary makes mention of the following important truth: You must do all you can to achieve this goal. Often times, the answer you will get will be in the form of inspiration. if that is the case, you need to act on it. You will be allowed to earn the victory.

6. *"Every good gift and every perfect gift is from above, and cometh down from the Father of lights"* - James 1:17 . Finally, understand who The Giver

actually is. The Secret is nebulous about this because it's a sensitive topic, but they elude to Him time and time again. The Giver is God, and it is by His generosity that all good things are accomplished.

You Tube

Title: **Eye to Eye: 'The Secret'**

Tags: CBS News eye to the secret Rev Michael Beckwith mainstream way of living

From: CBS

LEARN TO WALK, THEN WALK TO LEARN

You love walking. Instead of wheels, you'd rather take the "heel-toe express" and go for a long healthy stroll across town, right? Didn't think so. Everybody but the elderly thinks walking is L7, unfortunate considering the studies that show walking increases intelligence and comprehension. Learning through motion is called **kinaesthetic learning**, and theories like that of James J. Asher Ph.D., suggest that the way we learned as babies may be the best way to learn now - by internalizing literature and language with physical movements like walking.

To use a common example, a parent communicates via spoken language to the baby, and the baby responds with physical gestures in what's described as **language-body conversations**. Babies internalize and physically learn how language works *before they can even utter a word*. Since we all know how quickly babies learn and absorb new information, shouldn't we as adults be utilizing this natural and intuitive method of learning, and exercise our bodies at the same time?

As for the biomechanics, **here's why walking makes you smarter:**

Over 20% of all oxygen intake of the body is consumed by the brain, and when you furrow your brow in intense concentration, it's more. Now take the physical demands of walking, and oxygen intake goes up again and the brain becomes more alert, perceptive and functional. Depending on the intensity and duration, physical activity like walking can also trigger the secretion of the neurotransmitter serotonin (thereby further enhancing cognitive powers) and endorphins in the brain as well. In this heightened state, you'll have a better chance at understanding concepts and snagging easy-to-overlook details (provided you bring your reading with you). And yes, you'll look like a nerd. Bigtime.